Crisis at Columbia

CRISIS AT

COLUMBIA

REPORT OF THE
FACT-FINDING COMMISSION
APPOINTED TO INVESTIGATE
THE DISTURBANCES
AT COLUMBIA UNIVERSITY
IN APRIL AND MAY 1968

VINTAGE BOOKS
A Division of Random House
NEW YORK

First Vintage Edition, October 1968

CONTENTS

REPORT OF FACT-FINDING COMMISSION
ON COLUMBIA DISTURBANCES

PART ONE

CONDITIONS GIVING RISE TO THE DISTURBANCES

LIST OF ABBREVIATIONS

SDS	Students for a Democratic Society
SAS	Students Afro-American Society
SCC	Strike Coordinating Committee
SRO	Single Resident Occupancy
AHFG	Ad Hoc Faculty Group
Cit Council	Columbia College Citizenship Council

REPORT OF THE
FACT-FINDING COMMISSION
APPOINTED TO INVESTIGATE
THE DISTURBANCES
AT COLUMBIA UNIVERSITY
IN APRIL AND MAY 1968

INTRODUCTION

On May 4, 1968, the Executive Committee of the Faculties of Columbia University requested a Fact-Finding Commission to investigate and report on the disturbances on the campus during the week of April 23–30, 1968. The report was to cover (1) the chronology of events up to the intervention of the police and (2) the underlying causes of the disturbances. The Trustees of Columbia supported the Faculties' action. The Administration, headed by President Grayson Kirk and Vice-President David B. Truman, has given full cooperation. Many students and student organizations have cooperated. From the moment of its creation, however, the Commission became fully independent to chart its own course, conduct its own investigation, and reach its own conclusions.

The original members of the Commission were Archibald Cox, Professor of Law, Harvard University, Chairman; Hylan G. Lewis, Professor of Sociology, Brooklyn College; Simon H. Rifkind, formerly U.S. District Judge and currently a partner in the firm of Paul, Weiss, Goldberg, Rifkind, Wharton & Garrison; Dana L. Farnsworth, Director of Health Services, Harvard University, and Jefferson B. Fordham, Dean of the Law School, University of Pennsylvania. Dean Fordham withdrew almost at once, feeling that his previous public comments on the disturbances might give a misleading appearance of prejudgment. Anthony G. Amsterdam, Professor of Law, University of Pennsylvania, was named his successor.

The Commission has been assisted by a staff consisting of John S. Martin, Jr., as Counsel, Nicholas W. Fels, Assistant

Counsel, and Edward Skloot, Executive Director. In addition, Roger A. Lowenstein and David Kairys served as consultants on specific assignments. We are indebted to all these men for their support.

The investigation was conducted chiefly through formal testimony at public hearings. The Commission held 21 days of hearings and heard 79 witnesses. The transcript covers 3,790 pages. As time passed, it became apparent that less formal techniques would save time and provide information not otherwise available. Accordingly, the Commission supplemented the testimony with written statements and informal interviews, especially when dealing with background conditions and general impressions. In no instance have we relied upon a private communication to resolve a controverted issue of fact where inconsistent testimony is part of the open record.

Throughout the investigation the Fact-Finding Commission received complete cooperation from nearly all the individuals and organizations affected, including city officials, students, and members of the Columbia faculty and administration. We are especially grateful for the candor and honesty with which such major actors as Vice-President Truman and Professor Alan F. Westin reviewed tragic moments of stress.

Unfortunately, the Strike Coordinating Committee and the black students of Hamilton Hall resolved to boycott the Commission, challenging its "legitimacy" and utility, and distrusting its composition. Nevertheless, we have had considerable access to student viewpoints including radical student thinking. Individual students of almost every political persuasion have talked to us very freely about both the events and the underlying causes, including many who had active parts in the occupation of the buildings.

The effects of the formal boycott may be more serious in the case of the black students associated with the Students Afro-American Society (SAS), who led the demonstrators in Hamilton Hall. Until the end of summer they not only declined to make a formal appearance, but generally refused all our efforts to establish some form of informal or confidential communication. In mid-September, in response to an earlier invitation, SAS offered to read a prepared statement at a public hearing but stipulated that any questions should be put in writing so that any answers could first be debated at a full SAS meeting.° By then the Commission's report was too far advanced to take advantage of the proposed procedure.

We have been in touch with a few black students, however, and hope that this was an adequate check on the reports of other observers and some of our own inferences concerning the problems of black students at Columbia.†

°   °   °

Early in April 1968, the appearance of the Columbia campus was much like that of any large urban university. Columbia had experienced noisy political demonstrations but none equal to scenes at Berkeley, Wisconsin, or Michigan. Observers sensed an impending confrontation between the University officials and the more radical factions in the Students for a Democratic Society (SDS) who alone sought the confrontation and whose deliberately contemptuous manners had tended to freeze the Administration's response. Tension was rising; but on the whole, most observers would have said that the Columbia SDS was inept and ineffective. Outwardly, the Students Afro-American Society had not been active politically.

In the week of April 23–30, SDS and SAS led 700 to 1,000 students in the seizure of five university buildings. The students and their supporters barricaded themselves inside and defied the Administration. After six days, with the aid of more than 1,000 policemen, the buildings were reoccupied. But the campus was in chaos. For the rest of the academic year education was at a standstill (except at some professional schools), and a strike committee claimed the allegiance of many mem-

---

° This stipulation is consistent with standing policies of the SAS, which forbid any individual member to speak for the group, and requires that all statements made on its behalf be considered and approved at a meeting of the full group.

† Separate statement of Commission member Rifkind: "This Report has been developed through study and discussion by the members of the Commission and, as a whole, represents their combined judgment and general agreement. However, the specific findings in all their details and in the allocation of weight and emphasis do not necessarily bear my endorsement."

bers of the faculty as well as a vast number of students. The
fabric of the University's life is now twisted and torn. The
violence has now yielded to bitterness and distrust. Only
heroically open-minded and patient efforts can repair the injury.

The spark that set off the explosion was an SDS rally on
April 23, called to protest Columbia's relation to the Institute
for Defense Analyses (IDA), her "racist policies," and the Administration's placing six SDS leaders on probation for violation
of a rule against indoor demonstrations. But the spark, by itself,
seemed feeble; these were familiar issues and demonstrations
concerning them had never before aroused widespread indignation, much less challenged peace and reason.

What, then, were the conditions that composed such ex-
plosive tinder? What were the events leading from the rally
to the seizure of buildings? What caused so many students to
join the rebellion and to persevere so adamantly that the
University had to summon over 1,000 police officers in order
to clear the buildings, with attendant violence, chaos, and
bitterness that disrupted Columbia until the summer recess?

In addressing ourselves to these questions we deal first
with the underlying conditions that had come to exist by the
time of the SDS rally at the Sundial on April 23. We then
turn to the course of events as they led during the next six
days from the Sundial to police intervention, with all its tragic
consequences, including a second seizure of Hamilton Hall
and violent police action on May 21–22. In the third and final
portion of this report we state our general conclusions.

CONDITIONS GIVING RISE TO THE DISTURBANCES

COLUMBIA UNIVERSITY
The Center of The Morningside Campus

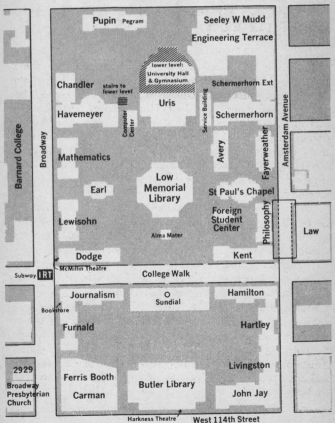

West 120th Street

Pupin   Pegram

Seeley W Mudd

Engineering Terrace

lower level:
University Hall
& Gymnasium

Chandler   stairs to lower level

Schermerhorn Ext

Uris

Service Building

Schermerhorn

Havemeyer   Computer Center

Barnard College

Broadway

Avery

Fayerweather

Mathematics

Low Memorial Library

Earl

St Paul's Chapel

Lewisohn

Foreign Student Center

Philosophy

Law

Alma Mater

Dodge

Kent

Subway IRT   McMillin Theatre

College Walk

Journalism

O
Sundial

Hamilton

Bookstore

Furnald

Hartley

2929
Broadway
Presbyterian
Church

Livingston

Ferris Booth

Butler Library

Carman

John Jay

Harkness Theatre   West 114th Street

Amsterdam Avenue

CONDITIONS GIVING RISE TO THE DISTURBANCES

Columbia is only one of a number of universities in different parts of the United States that have suffered violent student demonstrations. The University of California at Berkeley, Michigan, Wisconsin, Stanford, Howard, and San Francisco State are among the institutions that have experienced similar unrest. Seemingly analogous disturbances have also occurred in both eastern and western Europe. These facts alone are enough to suggest that conditions common to many universities were among the underlying causes of the explosion at Columbia.

The evidence we received confirms this inference. The evidence also shows that Columbia's special geographical situation tends to intensify many of the underlying factors. Yet it would be a mistake to conclude that Columbia experienced last spring's disturbances because she was caught in a broader movement beyond her control. Columbia's special geographical situation was plainly visible, and many of the resulting problems could have been faced. Other, more important ingredients of the mixture that exploded in April were faults resulting from Columbia's own organizational structure, from the attitudes of the faculty, and from the Administration's and Trustees' prior handling of matters of intense student concern, including problems involving increasingly self-conscious black students.

I

STUDENT ATTITUDES AND CONCERNS

A. General Characteristics

1. The present generation of young people in our universities is the best informed, the most intelligent, and the most idealistic this country has ever known. This is the experience of teachers everywhere.

It is also the most sensitive to public issues and the most sophisticated in political tactics. Perhaps because they enjoy the affluence to support their ideals, today's undergraduate and graduate students exhibit, as a group, a higher level of social conscience than preceding generations.

The ability, social consciousness and conscience, political sensitivity, and honest realism of today's students are a prime cause of student disturbances. As one student observed during our investigation, today's students take seriously the ideals taught in schools and churches, and often at home, and then they see a system that denies its ideals in its actual life. Racial injustice and the war in Vietnam * stand out as prime illustrations of our society's deviation from its professed ideals and of the slowness with which the system reforms itself. That they seemingly can do so little to correct the wrongs through conventional political discourse tends to produce in the most idealistic and energetic students a strong sense of frustration.

---

* See pp. 10–13.

Many of these idealists have developed with considerable sophistication the thesis that these flaws are endemic in the workings of American democracy. They argue that their form of pressure—direct action, confrontations, sit-ins, and (in some cases) physical violence—applied at points of institutional weakness, is a legitimate political tool comparable to the other forms of pressure—large political contributions, covert lobbying, favoritism, and the like—effectively applied by those who would lead society astray.*

For some of these students their universities have become surrogates for society. The university administration is close at hand. One can bedevil and strike out at it. If the frustrated activist cannot beat the system, he can at least insist that his own university should not lend itself to evil. There are a smaller number who see the university as a place of shelter untouched by the evils of society. They suffer profound shock when they find that the university, and therefore they as parts of it, are not so far removed. In their view this makes them guilty of complicity in profound social and moral evil.

2. Six thousand years ago an Egyptian priest carved on a stone the lament: "Our earth is degenerate . . . children no longer obey their parents." Impatience and antipathy for

---

* The argument of these students, stated in a little more detail, is as follows: Our governmental system, which in theory depends upon popular will, imperfectly expresses that will, because of the development of institutional failings of several sorts: for example, the political party system, the workings of influence and economic power, lobbying, and deficiencies in public education. As a result, when government and society are moving in tragically wrong-headed directions, these institutional weaknesses prevent recalling it to the true path by means within the tradition of political democracy. Direct action, confrontations, sit-ins, and (in some cases) physical violence applied at points of institutional weakness are political tools fairly comparable to the large political contributions, covert lobbying, favoritism, cocktail parties, and other *sub-rosa* power techniques used by the "Establishment." Such countervailing pressures either must be counted an acceptable part of the democratic process, or, if not, then American democracy is so far dead that its principles cannot be invoked as a restraint upon direct forms of action.

authority have always been hallmarks of youth, yet today one encounters the irony that this most promising of all student generations appears unusually antagonistic to all forms of restraint and peculiarly violent in social or political protest.

May not the fault lie with the older generation? Unless we are prepared to concede that ours is a sick society too corrupt to be saved, we must acknowledge that we have failed to transmit to many of the ablest young men and women either a sense of the values of reason, order, and civility or an appreciation of the fact that freedom depends upon voluntary restraint. We have managed to convey the idea that, because some of the values we upheld are outdated and others were always wrong, the remainder must also lack merit.

The sources of this shortcoming are not easily identified. One source may be our actual or seeming slowness and resistance to change where change is plainly required. Others may be inherent in our current civilization. The insight of the social sciences and the honesty of the arts have taught us to look at ourselves stripped of our pretense, and what we see is unlovely. We have the honesty and courage to see ourselves as we are, but perhaps, as Archibald MacLeish suggests, we lack the greater Hellenic courage to see man stumble and fall, yet avow his nobler capacity. It became unfashionable among forward-looking intellectuals 30 or 40 years ago to speak of progress, virtue, and wisdom, or to examine the supports on which they rest.

Size and complexity, as elsewhere in modern life, enormously increase the difficulties of communication and response. The growing demands of each teacher's own field of knowledge and the opportunities for applying it in government and industry divert him from close personal intercourse with his students. (Paradoxically, it is usually the teacher actively engaged in applying his knowledge to society who is most interesting to the largest number of students.)

It is sometimes said the schools and colleges exert too much pressure upon students. In the case of many seemingly irrelevant scholastic requirements there may be something to the charge. Certainly the intense busy-ness that afflicts both faculty and students discourages easy discourse and diminishes the quality of personal relations. Yet the problem is not so much one of pressure as of pressure for the wrong things. Many students are not being given responsibilities which sufficiently challenge their capabilities. The formal structure of most universities is authoritarian and paternalistic in relation to students, and it often excludes even the faculty from important aspects of university policy. Columbia inherited more than its share of this style. Bringing students closer into a community of all the parts of a university, including the process of decision-making, would promote that intimate exchange of ideas and experiences which is vital to maturity. It would also aid them in learning how to control rapidly changing technological, social, and cultural conditions.

The last point is best illustrated by the unfortunate alienation of the older graduate students and youngest faculty members—those who have only recently finished their own formal training or who are still in that intermediate stage of being half-student, half-faculty member. They are in a peculiarly advantageous position to help bridge the gap between generations. When they feel aggrieved, misunderstood, or exploited, they understandably ally themselves with any other elements within the institution that are unhappy and desirous of change. When communication between them and their more influential (and usually older) colleagues in the faculty and administration becomes attenuated and when they are denied effective participation in decisions that are vital to them, political tactics based upon muscle may become an appealing substitute for reasonable discussion. This factor was plainly evident during the April disturbances at Columbia where many of the junior faculty took parts encouraging to students in the buildings.

When decisions are made largely on the basis of who has the most power, especially when power is concentrated in a formal authoritarian structure, more and more people within the institution will be dissatisfied. When the decisions are made after full and frank discussion of the various issues involved, and with all opinions being taken into consideration, cohesion develops and effective teaching about the ways in which a democracy should operate is possible—in fact, an actual demonstration takes place. The radical demonstrations for "student

power" illustrate what can occur when thoughtful groups
trained to criticize and dissent are forced into the tactics of
manipulation instead of the rational correction of defects in
education and research.

3. During the years in which the present university students were in secondary school the gap between the generations was widened by marked changes in speech, conduct,
dress, and manners. Although older people generally disap-
proved the changes, the more exaggerated the new styles
became the more they were promoted by entertainers and
influential mass media. The cycle became self-sustaining. Inflated rhetoric and violence began to spread through contemporary society—again largely because the mass media give
them the greatest attention. Among the young, inflated rhetoric
and bizarre personal appearance have become symbolic behavior indicating disapproval of the "Establishment" and the
older generation. As the number of late adolescents and young
adults increased in relation to older people, the young became
increasingly aware of their power if only they were willing to
reject conventional restraints.

The conflicts of style and removal of customary restraints
breed antagonisms and even distrust; thus, they increase the
tendency to resolve problems by strongly emotional and often
intolerant lines of action. And, to a degree, even violent obstruction (as in April) becomes a form of generational self-
expression.

4. The size and complexity of the large universities in an
urban society increase the alienation of students and, as we
shall see, there is too little at Columbia to offset the feeling.
One form of response, which must be mentioned among the
causes of violent demonstrations, is the romantic reaction
against complexity, rationality, and restraint, which has become
a small but pervasive thread in student life.

In philosophy, it is illustrated by the popularity of Anarch-
ism.

In politics, the appeal of rigid doctrine with simple explanations becomes irresistible. A simplistic demonology pur-
portedly describing the "Establishment" that controls "the
system" comes to explain all the hardships and injustices re-

sulting from the complex cross-currents of a technological society and the selfishness and blundering awkwardness of man. Che Guevara and Frantz Fanon have become folk-heroes for some radicals. Others wait for the day when the students will be joined by proletarian workers in a Marxist (or Maoist) revolution.

At Columbia more than a few students saw the barricading of the buildings in April as the moment when they began meaningful lives. They lived gloriously like revolutionary citizens of Paris. They liberated buildings and flew the Red flag. Men and women shared alike without restraint. The marriage ceremony performed in a liberated building by a chaplain attached to the University symbolized the glorious moments of truth. Later, a graduate student, asked to explain to us why he had joined in the seizure, replied that, although he had participated in civil rights activities and every possible peace demonstration, all had come to nothing, but in April, in the buildings, he and others knew that at last they were taking effective action for things worthwhile. The mixture of political and social romanticism varied widely from individual to individual. Many took part without political motivation.

Obviously, romanticism is only one form—probably a minor form—of response to the gap between social and political ideals and social and political performance. Many students who join in civil disobedience, direct action, and other forms of obstructive protest see their tactics as necessary catalysts of social reform in an age when conventional political methods have proved inadequate. The sit-down strikes of 1937–38 and the sit-in demonstrations of the civil rights movement are cited as proof that, whatever the legality or illegality of obstructive tactics, "they work." °

These general characteristics of student attitudes are intensified at Columbia by the urban environment and the conditions of student life. We discuss these problems later.† Here it is enough to point out that Columbia's student body,

---

° For further discussion of this aspect of the background of the upheaval, see pp. 25–29.

† See pp. 30–33.

while less radical than others in its activities, is probably among the most politically sophisticated and liberal. This is the result partly of tradition, partly of environment, and partly of the processes of selection (including self-selection among high school students).

At Columbia, as at other universities, students' opinions cover the entire spectrum of political life. But two issues command unusually broad agreement among the young and engage their deepest emotions: the peace movement and racial justice. Both were causes of the April disturbances.

B. *The War in Vietnam*

During Dr. Truman's testimony he observed:

> Some of us have felt for a very long time that if it were inescapable that the current war in Vietnam had to continue on, it was debatable whether university communities could survive, because the tension is not only among students but in faculties, and the whole fabric of the institution is strained.
>
> In a sense, I think there have been two battlefields in the war. One in Vietnam, and the other on our university campuses. And they are not good places for battlefields.

The Vietnam war is the overriding concern of nearly all students. For them it is a matter of life or death—to kill or be killed. For many, it is an immoral war and all who support it are immoral; it should be stopped at once—how stopped is a detail irrelevant to men of commitment. The consensus among students and most of the vocal intellectual community appears to validate their criticism, hence differing opinions are condemned with earnest righteousness.

The uncertainties of the draft, moreover, and the overbrooding threat of nuclear warfare have intensified every grievance and frustration.

Student opposition to the war has many forms. Student activists have taken part in nearly all the peace and anti-draft demonstrations. Just as some learned the tactics of obstructive protest in the civil rights movement others gained experience in rallies at draft boards and recruiting stations.*

The university became the focus of both criticism and frustration wherever it could be linked with the defense establishment; in furnishing class rankings to draft boards, in making facilities available for ROTC programs, in permitting recruitment for the Armed Forces or war-related industries, and in government research. Militant young men and women, frustrated by their inability to shape a vastly complex society upon an issue that seems both moral and simple, turn to make their weight felt on nearer and more vulnerable institutions. On the war, therefore, even more than on other issues, the university becomes a surrogate for society and the New Left has evolved political theories asserting that the university is a microcosm of society in order to rationalize the transference. Many large universities—Wisconsin, Michigan, and Harvard among others—have experienced seriously obstructive demonstrations against their alleged complicity in the war in Vietnam.

Students at Columbia appear typical of the students at other large universities in these respects. The opposition to the war is more vocal, perhaps, than in the south and parts of the midwest, but it is not discernibly different from other universities in the northeast or on the west coast.

Militant groups have lashed out at Columbia, as elsewhere. Although the demonstrations were neither as large nor as disruptive as others, Columbia experienced at least her numerical share of incidents as the fighting in Vietnam intensified. In May 1965, violence broke out, which the City police were called to suppress, when protesters formed a human chain to block the Naval Reserve Officers Training Corps from entering Low Library † in order to hold final review ceremonies. On November 15, 1966, 200 students, organized by SDS,

---

* We do not suggest that obstructive protest has been in any sense characteristic of either the civil rights or peace movements. Such tactics were exceptional and, at least in the civil rights movement, even those exceptions were usually associated with the unconstitutional suppression of other forms of expression.

† Low Library is the central administration building at Columbia. It is no longer used as a library.

marched into Dodge Hall in order to "ask a few questions" of
a recruiter for the Central Intelligence Agency (CIA) who
was interviewing prospective applicants for employment. One
day later, on November 16, 150 students marched to President
Kirk's office in Low Library with a letter demanding an official statement of non-cooperation with the CIA. In February
1967, 18 students engaged in a sit-in demonstration, blocking
access to the rooms in Dodge Hall where CIA interviews were
to be conducted. On April 20, 1967, 300 SDS members and sympathizers filled the lobby of John Jay Hall where recruiters
for the U.S. Marine Corps had set up tables. The next day
800 anti-recruiting demonstrators milled about Van Am Quadrangle, together with 500 counter-demonstrators sympathetic
to campus recruiting. On February 28, 1968, a 200-man picket
line, sponsored by SDS, marched toward Low Library in protest of the presence of recruiters for Dow Chemical Company;
80 Barnard and Columbia students left the march to stage a
sit-in demonstration in Dodge Hall. On March 27, 1968, SDS
led more than 100 students in a march through Low Library
in a demonstration against the Institute for Defense Analyses.

We list these incidents here simply to show that issues
connected with the Vietnam war had repeatedly stirred large
demonstrations prior to last April's disturbances. By then,
attention had focused upon Columbia's connection with the
Institute for Defense Analyses. The connection was emphasized beyond its intrinsic importance, but it became a symbol
of Columbia's participation in the war for many critics of the
national policy in Vietnam. As such, it was manifestly an ex-
plosive issue.*

C. Civil Rights and Community Relations

The cause of racial justice, more than any other issue,
brought students out of the political lethargy of the 1950's and,
like the Vietnam war, engrossed their deepest emotions. Today
the "racism" they condemn encompasses not only active racial
discrimination but continued acquiescence in the poverty, the
denial of opportunity, and the human suffering that segrega-

---

* The issue is discussed in detail at pp. 89–95.

tion in ghettos make integral parts of the Negro and Puerto Rican experience. Racial issues and the war on poverty also engage the active support of a larger segment of the student body than any other issue, with the possible exception of the war in Vietnam. At Columbia the presence of racial issues, symbolized by the projected gymnasium in Morningside Park, undoubtedly had much to do with the breadth of the faculty and student support for those who sparked the April uprising.

Columbia's location epitomizes the conflicts and intensifies the emotional commitments and frustrations of the movement to relieve racism and poverty. Situated on Morningside Heights, the University looks down on the flats of Harlem, one of the most depressed of all urban ghettos. Millions of black people must have looked up at the institutional buildings as symbols of the affluence of a white society; remote, unattainable, and indifferent. Hundreds of Columbia students who came to the University and then went down into Harlem with high ideals of social justice, but little prior experience with the realities of urban poverty, have been shocked by immersion in the ghetto. Not only the strongest criticism of the projected gymnasium but also important support for the seizure of the buildings came from the College Citizenship Council whose members were actively in touch with Columbia's poorest neighbors.° A University official suggested that the response of these students was a case of well-intentioned but naive overreaction. Many of us have also come to acquiesce in "the realities," with more or less discomfort, but one wonders whether the sensitive students' perception is not closer to the truth.

D. Grievances and Problems of Black Students

One of the outstanding features of the most recent wave of university demonstrations has been the central role of self-

---

° The Citizenship Council is engaged in important social service programs and other forms of community assistance in the Morningside and Harlem areas. Many students contribute time and energy to these activities and thus are drawn into continuous contact with the local areas.

conscious black students. Especially within the past year, Negro students on campuses, large and small, throughout the country have made unprecedented efforts to bring about changes in campus life increasing their participation and enhancing respect for their identity. Their goals included changes in curriculum, personnel, admissions, and living conditions. Sometimes they worked alone as more or less organized black students, sometimes in loose, temporary coalition with predominantly white organizations. Always they were moved by an intensely self-conscious design to act as black students and to make "black" a proud symbol. Indeed, a recent accomplishment, mainly attributable to Negro college youth, is the unprecedented semantic reversal of the negative racial connotations formerly associated with the words "Negro" and especially "black."

Similarly, there is reason to think that the role of the black students at Columbia was uniquely important, for it may well have been their decision to request the white demonstrators to leave Hamilton Hall that converted a somewhat unfocused, noisy, disorderly, all-night demonstration into an unprecedented uprising involving the occupation of five campus buildings.

In analyzing the particular grievances and problems of black students as related to the April disturbances, one must first note the importance of their perceptions and experiences of their contemporary environment, some long-standing and some recent, some general and some unique to Columbia. Thus, black students have been profoundly influenced by, and react sharply to, shifts in the civil rights movement, just as they are extraordinarily sensitive to the political and cultural meanings and uses of race in contemporary society. The much publicized generation gap may well have even more effect upon black youths than others, for they are keenly aware that the movement for changes in the status of the Negro has been spearheaded by the young, especially by the initiative and energy of self-conscious, and increasingly race-conscious, Negroes in college. Public issues, such as the Vietnam war, the youth movement, and the worsening crisis of the ghettos, concern them no less than socially conscious white students, and probably not very differently except where their concern is racially self-conscious or influenced by a rather sophisticated awareness of the identity yet separateness of the demands being made by and for Negroes, the poor, and the young.

Thus, as students at Columbia, the black students are affected like all other students by their perceptions of the quality of student life and the apparent attitudes toward students of both faculty and Administration. Yet, even while they share this important degree of common experience with others, black students are uniquely influenced by their perception of the manner in which Columbia has dealt with small but successive generations of Negro students.

Historically, the enrollment of Negro students at Columbia has been very small, and those few have been isolated in different schools. Recently, Columbia, like a number of other Ivy League colleges where competition for admission is keen, has made serious and successful efforts to increase the enrollment of black students. Some of them come with a markedly different preparation from the rest of the student body. Their social, economic, and educational backgrounds create very real practical problems of adjustment. Yet nothing effective is offered to ease the transition. Until this is changed, the more that is done to enable promising young men from rural areas or urban ghettos to obtain a university education, the deeper the dilemma grows.

We do not imply that the black student body of Columbia is homogeneous in terms of class, income, or educational achievement. As among the white students, grievances, protest, and political consciousness (and black consciousness in the case of the Negro) bear no necessary relationship to cultural, economic, or educational advantages. In the recent past and now, middle-class black students have been among the leaders of protest.

One experience common to all backgrounds, however, has been the impression that Columbia is a discriminating, indifferent, frequently hostile world, just because it is dominated and peopled by whites. Even the instruction and curriculum emphasize that black students are moving into another man's world. Black students are a small minority. There are very few, if any, black deans, black professors, or black instructors with whom to identify. The courses ignore the history and culture of black people. The curriculum often strikes them, like other students, as irrelevant, perhaps more because its relevance is not made clear than because it is actually irrelevant. The shortness with which these basic facts can be stated must not be allowed to obscure either their reality or substantive importance.

Often the situations that bother students grow out of the very efforts to remedy past injustices. A Columbia undergraduate wryly gave this insight into one kind of situation that affects self-image. In substance, he said: "We know that we are admitted to Ivy League colleges, although we would not make it under normal standards of admissions policy, because black people engaged in demonstrations, rioted, and otherwise pressured the white establishment. This tells us we are not up to the competition—at least by those standards. At the same time, the knowledge lessens our incentive for academic achievement. This seems to say that the same pressures will get us into law schools and other graduate study regardless of our achievement." The student who made this statement had too good judgment to mean it without many qualifications. The ability of black students is high, and most would be accepted under a suitable standard. The point, needless to say, is not whether the statement is absolutely true, rather that the creeping doubt or kernel of truth probably created in him or his fellows both some insecurity and some frustration.

There are still evidences of apparent prejudice. Some fraternities appear still to discriminate against black students. Occasional incidents have arisen involving restrictions imposed by the national, parent organization. Sometimes, uncomfortable feeling arises at mixers. At Columbia, the security guards were long allowed to follow the unforgivable practice of inspecting black students' identification cards when they entered college buildings although the white students were passed without notice. (Later Vice-President David B. Truman halted the practice.)

The black student is also currently under another set of

psychological pressures that comes from both the resurgence
of social consciousness in youth and from the Black Power
movement. He feels a conscious obligation to help the less fortunate and a subconscious pressure to prove his militancy. His
reaction may be increased by a sense that he is enjoying education and opportunities denied to many less fortunate Negroes.

At Columbia, the Negro students had not shown signs of
collective militancy until rather recently. One incident of record was the seizure of 1,500 copies of an issue of the *Jester*—
the student-humor magazine—in the spring of 1967, upon the
ground that it contained an article offensive to the Negro race.
Columbia's black students took little visible part in the increasing number of protest demonstrations against the projected
gymnasium in Morningside Park through 1966, 1967, and the
first three months of 1968. Some of them must have been
troubled by the contrast between their own seeming indifference and the active efforts of white students who joined civil
rights and other organizations in Harlem in demonstrations
seeking to block the construction.

The complex responses of black students in the April events
were suggested in added dimension by a close observer who
was discussing the black students' seizure and barricading of
Hamilton Hall. Among other things, he stressed the aim of
Negro students to be taken seriously as people:

> What was the cause? Whether they would accept it or not,
> I believe their basic couse was to dramatize the unrespon-
> siveness of the University, primarily to them. But that's
> not easily sold or easily acceptable to [one's own] con-
> sciousness.
>
> The more acceptable way of selling that [to oneself]
> would be [to speak of] the unresponsiveness of the Uni-
> versity to the community and to its very real needs; and in
> doing that, they get an extra dividend. They demonstrate
> their identification—the students' identification—with the
> community to which the University is unresponsive. What-
> ever guilt they may [feel] about having advantages which
> the average kid of their age in Harlem doesn't have, is

somewhat ameliorated by this action which is—to take their phrase—"for the black brothers in the ghetto." And they get publicity while they do it.

Q. Earlier, when you were asked about the motivation for the demonstration in Hamilton Hall, you replied in much better chosen words than I have, that the aim was to be taken seriously as people, to be responded to as people, to be recognized and to have the University respond in a meaningful way. I was wondering if one raised the same question about the students in the other buildings, whether the answer would be just the same.

A. It would be identical, but fundamentally similar . . . The difference would be probably in the complexities. In the case of the Negro students in Hamilton Hall, another ingredient would be that, by this act, they were demonstrating they were part of the movement, and "movement" is very important. Such action helps to deal with guilt, too, not being the privileged Negroes, pets of the white establishment but as militant as Malcolm, Stokely, and Rap.

The black students who occupied Hamilton Hall were not unmindful of the complexities of the gymnasium controversy, although they also saw the symbolic racial issue. But they were most consciously concerned with the demonstration of their power, for the very practical reasons already noted.

II

UNCERTAINTY CONCERNING THE ROLE OF THE UNIVERSITY

In examining the conditions of student life which make for unrest at American universities it is important not to overlook the fact that the universities themselves are in a state of transition where they, consciously or unconsciously, face exceedingly complex yet fundamental issues concerning their functions and curriculum. The lack of accepted answers to such basic questions not only impairs institutional cohesion within the university as a whole, it also promotes student dissatisfaction and unrest.

Although we lack any special insight into the nature of these problems—indeed, most of us would disclaim the qualifications for dealing with them—still it seems important to say enough to illustrate the connection between the disturbances and the uncertainties concerning the universities' role in current society.

A. *The Role of the University in Relation to Society*

The increasing complexity and sophistication of all aspects of the industrial and social order have enormously increased the demands upon universities to join in applying to practical uses the knowledge, skills, and equipment they assemble. State and federal governments, industry, foundations, and community organizations are constantly calling upon individual professors for active participation in action programs as well as for expert opinion; and both the professors and their institutions value the opportunity. Universities, as others have said, have become knowledge factories with much wider and possibly more powerful constituencies than the students whom they educate. At least some branches of the university, moreover, are attracting to their faculties a new type of academician—the man of action as well as intellect whose interest is not the pursuit of truth for its own sake but to shape society from a vantage point combining academic security, intellectual weapons, and political action.

The trend raises questions of extraordinary difficulty, of which we mention only two.

1. What is the proper role of the university in the immediate practical application of knowledge to military, industrial, social, and economic problems? During the hearings before this Commission it was suggested that Columbia's relations with her neighbors would be immeasurably improved if, instead of buying up SRO buildings and driving the tenants from the vicinity, the University would bring the expertise of her doctors and social scientists to the aid of those unfortunate occupants who resorted to crime, prostitution, and drugs.* Witnesses also urged that West Harlem affords endless opportunities for the School of Social Work to do work of immeasurable aid to the community.

Perhaps the answer is that the universities must expand in these directions, but the expansion will not be without costs. Since the time, energy, and money diverted from pure research at universities will not be replaced anywhere else in society, the diversion of academic resources would limit the seeds of progress. Furthermore, without radical revision of curriculum and methods of instruction, the professors so engaged would have still less time than today for work and informal association with students.

2. If universities are to be actively engaged in social en-

---

* See pp. 36–41.

deavor, how and by whom are decisions to be made concerning when, how, where, and to what uses their knowledge shall be applied? Choices have to be made: there are not enough hours and resources to go around and often the alternatives conflict with one another. Moreover, the more the application of knowledge brings the university into involvement with society, the more apparent it becomes that the choices depend on judgments of social and political policy. When students see work being done at a university on the application of science to spreading death and destruction in Vietnam, but little evidence of similar work on eliminating poverty and racial injustice, they are naturally concerned about the decision-making process. Are the choices left to individual professors? If so, are the choices really left to them? What if their political decisions seem badly mistaken?

Making decisions on the application of its knowledge to society must, to some degree, politicize the university. One is thus forced to inquire how politicization of the centers of knowledge affects pursuit of the ideal of detached, objective search for truth. And this leads back to the initial question concerning the university's role in the application of knowledge.

B. *The Curriculum*

Students are widely dissatisfied with the formal educational curriculum of American universities. That dissatisfaction, although not assigned by students as a ground for the April disturbances, undoubtedly helped to make them sufficiently restless for other motives to stir them into joining the uprising. Thus, many of the students who occupied Fayerweather Hall had long been critical of the educational offerings of their respective departments and some had earnestly sought discussion and change. Immediately after the police action and in subsequent weeks, most schools and departments quickly established joint faculty-student panels whose efforts were to be devoted, in part, to a review of curricular questions. Large numbers of students and faculty realized that if the curriculum (which is the students' chief contact with the university) seems "irrelevant" or worse, the student is bound to ask why he should worry about maintaining the university against hostile assault.

The central educational assignment of American colleges and universities has long been to prepare functionally effective people for rather definite roles in industry, finance, government, and the established professions. The young man whose motivation parallels accepted categories of career, status, and prestige has little reason to question the universities' curricular offerings or performance; they do this preparatory job exceedingly well, and often give the individual lasting scholarly or cultural interests.

But the simple fact is that a constantly growing proportion of the best students does not look forward to careers molded along the established lines of professional or business success. The point can be proved statistically, but it is enough to illustrate it by reference to the tremendous interest in social service work and the Peace Corps and, conversely, to the difficulties established business firms and their professional advisers now face in recruiting.* Although most professors will rush to deny that their offerings are in any sense vocational, one suspects that a good many of the vocal complaints of the irrelevance of the curriculum are attributable to the fact that the kind of education offered by our colleges and universities has not changed as sharply as the interests of the most vocal and energetic students. One cannot help being impressed by the enormous enthusiasm that goes into "liberation schools" and extra-curricular as well as "anti-curricular" offerings.

One also wonders whether the charge of "irrelevance" that

---

* We have been referred to a most provocative paper dealing with Columbia College students, written by Mr. Stanley Raffel, now a graduate student in the Department of Sociology. In the paper he notes the disturbing fact that, although almost half the freshman class entering in selected years intended to enter the *academic* profession, by graduation the number had dropped to a little more than one-sixth. Mr. Raffel apparently concludes that the Columbia College environment actually turns academically motivated college students toward professional careers as a second or third choice.

both undergraduate and graduate students level at the cur-, riculum is not a way of challenging a mode or style of academic life that has remained unchanged at the core since the nineteenth century, or—some will say—since the earliest European universities. The revolutionary changes in technological and social conditions, the vastly different composition of student bodies, and the enormously increased opportunities for human attainment may well require equally radical changes in the university scholar.

One other source of student disappointment in the university should be noted. Perhaps because of less certainty about their status, career goals, and broader aspirations, perhaps for much more complex reasons, more sensitive and intelligent students than formerly are looking to the university to help them discover what life is about. Yet most of these are disappointed. Too little of the whole elaborate paraphernalia of academic activities appears to be concerned with the conduct of a man's life. J. D. Salinger's Franny gives this insight:

> I don't think it would have all got me quite so down if just once in a while—just *once* in a while—there was at least some polite little *perfunctory* implication that knowledge *should* lead to *wisdom*, and that if it *doesn't*, it's just a disgusting waste of time! But there never is! You never even hear any *hints* dropped on a campus that wisdom is *supposed* to be the goal of knowledge. You hardly ever even hear the word "wisdom" mentioned! Do you want to hear something really funny? In almost four years of college—and this is the absolute truth—in almost four years of college, the only time I can remember ever even hearing the expression "wise man" being used was in my freshman year, in Political Science! And you know how it was used? It was used in reference to some nice old poopy elder statesman who'd made a fortune in the stock market and then gone to Washington to be an adviser to President Roosevelt. I'm not saying that happens to everybody, but I just get so upset when I think about it I could die.*

---

* J. D. Salinger, *Franny and Zooey* (Bantam Books), pp. 146–147.

We do not mean to imply that the proportion of students who are worried about wisdom and therefore share Franny's disappointment is high. We know many teachers who help their students toward the understanding of life's unanswerable questions, not so much by precept as by example. One witness suggested to us, perhaps with more than a touch of irony, that no one should be so foolish as to look to a university to help him discover what life is about. But, despite the doubts and qualifications, it seems to us that the university should not be allowed to remain that "irrelevant" to the questing student, if only because there is presently no other institution that claims all knowledge as its province. Until such students are more convincingly shown that universities are addressing themselves to such questions, their disappointment will remain at least a latent source of disaffection.

III

SOCIAL ATTITUDES TOWARD DISRUPTIVE DEMONSTRATIONS

The forms in which student protests find expression are nor-mally affected, in marked degree, by the social and moral judg-ments of a wider community. For even if those judgments were wholly rejected by most students—and they are not—still they would be operative facts with which the student leaders must deal as a matter of tactics. Thus, one of the conditions con-tributing to the April disturbances at Columbia was the preva-lent moral uncertainty over the acceptability of the seizure of buildings as a means of influencing reform.

The past decade has seen a marked change in attitudes toward the acceptability of disobedience, harassment, and physical obstruction as methods of influencing social and polit-ical action. Tactics that would have been so widely condemned 10 or 15 years ago as to be self-defeating are now accepted and approved in many quarters as moral endeavors to achieve worthy ends. This is especially true among political liberals and youth. The spreading use of such tactics and the much, much wider spirit of tolerance toward their use not only in-creased the likelihood of resort to physical seizure and occupa-tion of buildings but enabled the rebels to escape unanimous condemnation and gain widespread support among students and faculty once the seizure occurred.

We need scarcely recall the national events in the civil

rights movement that spread tolerance for passive disobedience of unjust laws, then for deliberate confrontation with officials enforcing arguably unconstitutional restrictions upon freedom of expression, and finally for the tactics of physical obstruction and harassment as means of influencing policy. The sequence began with the bus boycott in Montgomery, Alabama. It spread next to the sit-in demonstrations at segregated lunch counters and restaurants. Later, there were instances of plain physical obstruction such as completely blocking the entrances to restaurants or crowding into libraries. Student activists gained first-hand experience with such tactics when they went into the south, and later into the northern urban ghettos, to work for racial equality. They could not fail to observe the effectiveness of the tactics, both in dramatizing a cause and in compelling concessions. Any moral or legal scruples were overwhelmed by the morality of the objective. There was virtually no condemnation of their action in segments of the community interested in reform.

Disruption, harassment, and physical obstruction then became common tactics in the peace movement, in which student leaders everywhere played dedicated roles. Again, although more doubts were expressed, there was no general outcry that the tactic was intolerable regardless of its goal.

Thus, the use of disruptive indoor demonstrations and sit-ins as methods of student protest against university policy—at least in relation to the black community or the war in Vietnam—resulted from the progressive extension of tactics encouraged by many moral and political leaders. Careful thought makes it plain that distinctions can, and probably should, be drawn. The Montgomery bus boycott involved neither physical obstruction nor disobedience to law. The sit-ins, at least where there was no physical interference with other patrons, involved the bona fide claim of a constitutional right to service in the lunch counter or restaurant. Both are a far cry from the seizure of buildings as a way of forcing action upon other issues, and from physical harassment or obstruction of others' activities as a means of compelling concessions. But the distinctions, vital as they are, were usually overlooked and the tactics lumped loosely under such heads as "civil disobedience," "non-violence," and "direct action." No one should be greatly surprised, therefore, that students, accustomed to the acceptability of one, should move gradually into the other. Nor is it altogether strange, in this milieu, that the crowded occupation of a college building by 250 protesting students was spontaneously converted into a sit-down, and then a seizure with barricaded doors.

It seems quite plain that, in April, there was no consensus on the Columbia campus that condemned the tactics of disruptive demonstrations.* Columbia has a proud tradition of freedom of expression. Even as the demonstrations grew more strident and then more obstructive during 1966 and 1967, the Administration itself usually leaned toward tolerance (although once or twice it sought to draw a tighter line). Other members of the University community in position to have strong influence on its standards of acceptable conduct provided social and moral support. During the April disturbances, a clergyman attached to the Columbia community married two students in Fayerweather Hall during the period of student occupation. The support of this religious counselor and another contributed to the escalation and duration of the disorders by conferring an appearance of moral legitimacy. The Ad Hoc Faculty Group (AHFG) not only offered to disrupt the University by calling a faculty strike as a substitute for the students' physical occupation of the buildings; it also resolved to enforce its will by physical obstruction in the event that the Administration chose to clear the building by the normal processes of law.† The threat was repeated in modified language

---

* In using such terms as "disruptive demonstrations" and "physical harassment or obstructions," we do not mean to prescribe a code of conduct. We have in mind not only the seizure and barricading of buildings but also other means of physically preventing, or seriously hampering, the normal activities of others in the community as a means of protesting or inducing action, whether the physical obstruction is violent or non-violent. The core of meaning seems quite clear even though there is a shadowy area around the fringes where minor physical inconvenience may be justifiable in the interests of expression.

† Paragraph 4 of the resolution of April 25, 1968 stated: "Until this crisis is settled, we will stand before the occupied buildings to prevent forcible entry by police or others."

in an effort to induce the Administration to accept the AHFG proposals for settlement. Nice distinctions can be drawn and subtleties of meaning were doubtless intended. Nevertheless, such incidents both reveal and help to create a climate in which even the physical seizure and occupancy of buildings is not seen as an intolerable offense against the entire University community.

To observe the climate is not to approve it. For reasons stated below * we are convinced that any resort to physical harassment or obstruction as means of influencing the policies and specific decisions of a university is as intolerable as the attitude that policies affecting the public stance of a university are not the concern of faculty or students.

Nor do we suggest that the acceptance of physical harassment and obstruction as a permissible expression of dissent was the unanimous, or even the majority, view of either faculty or students. The point is simply that the largely accidental conversion of a disruptive demonstration into the physical occupancy and barricading of buildings by more than 750 students was made markedly easier, and their refusal to leave voluntarily was stiffened, by the failure of many high-minded liberals to develop the necessary distinctions among the kinds of conduct often too loosely lumped together as "direct action" or "civil disobedience."

Our judgment that such conduct is unacceptable in a free university may provoke the debate. We appreciate the need for rethinking a question that has been thrown into confusion by the strong forces of social reform. The essence of our finding is that one of the causes of the April disturbances was the failure of the academic community to think out the implication of many current forms of political demonstration and to build a firm consensus of moral opinion concerning the limits upon morally acceptable methods of expressing dissent.†

---

* See pp. 196–197.

† Individual statement of Commission member Amsterdam: "Terms such as 'disruption' and 'physical obstruction' cover a range of differing kinds of conduct. I can go along with our definitions of the terms for our present purposes without attempting

fine precision or exacting analysis, because we do not undertake to propose a code of permissible forms of dissent but rather to state the urgent need for hard thinking and lucid debate within the academic community that may lay an informed foundation for fair consensus relative to the appropriate limitations upon conduct expressing dissent on the campus. I trust that, in the course of that debate, our language will not be misunderstood, nor our definitions misapplied, to settle issues finer than we set our sights on. Specifically, I do not read our text as saying that every demonstration activity which produces any disruption or entails any physical obstruction is thereby condemnable; nor as undertaking to say exactly when, where, how, or by whom, what particular degree of disruption or physical obstruction becomes condemnable. Nor will we be read, I hope, as saying that demonstration conduct which is not in itself condemnable may nevertheless be condemned because it is a step in the direction of the line of condemnable disruption and obstruction, and by this step creates an atmosphere in which heedless and uncritical thought more readily accepts further and other steps that do go over the line."

IV

CONDITIONS SPECIAL TO COLUMBIA

The forces of unrest common to students at many large universities are themselves sufficient to create appreciable risk of demonstrations resembling the April outbreak at Columbia. The degree of the risk, the violence of the explosion, and the duration of the conflict at Columbia were all increased, however, by elements in the University's own condition and the conduct of her affairs.

We have already noted how the University's location tends to magnify the forces of unrest. This portion of our report calls attention to elements in Columbia's structure and style that left her deficient in the cement that binds a university into a cohesive unit. We also point out how the coincidence of disruptive issues at Columbia occurred at a time when the members of the University seemed to have lost some of the sense of self-confident participation in a common enterprise, whose welfare had first claim on their loyalty.

A. Student Life

Columbia's urban location lessens the coherence of the student body and weakens students' sense of identification with the institution. The competing attractions of an exciting metropolitan area—which are among the great values Columbia provides for her students—nevertheless operate as centrifugal forces. The size and impersonality of the city enhance the size and impersonality of the University in relation to the individual, and both may nourish the feeling of powerless anonymity that leads to alienation, frustration, and resentment.

The coherence and *esprit* of a student body are profoundly affected by the quality of student life. The formal testimony and our informal conversations largely confirm the description supplied us by a psychologist who served five years on the Columbia College Counseling Service and one year as acting director:

"On a tour of inspection of all of the campus dormitories with the Director of Men's Residence Halls, I discovered that despite the pleasing, esthetically interesting ground floor public rooms of the older men's dorms, the actual residence facilities for the men were appallingly restricted. Two men would be housed in a room barely adequate for one—consisting of a double decker bed, one desk, one chair, and one bureau. Although some rooms were larger, the majority of students were housed in the manner I have just described. Naked light bulbs in corridors, scarred and battered furniture, walls, and floors give the older dormitories the general atmosphere of a run-down rooming house. Since most of the Columbia students came from middle-class or upper middle-class families, this was a rather striking comedown for them. However, as we know where there is a social *esprit de corps,* University facilities *per se* are not terribly important. However, at Columbia there was neither group feeling nor individual comfort. Frequently students reported a sense that they were being exploited for the financial profit of the University.

"On individual residence floors there were no social or recreational facilities that would permit a few boys to congregate. At our suggestion there was an experiment in which one ordinarily income-producing room on one floor was converted into a student lounge. Although students on that floor reported greater satisfaction with their experience at the College than they had experienced previously, and although the residence hall counselor reported less vandalism than on other floors previous to the changes, as far as I know this provision of social facilities on each floor was never made part of the routine dormitory program. Carman Hall was the newest dormitory on campus, constructed along a corridor plan with small lounges at either end of extremely long and barren corridors. The social rooms were in no way integrated with the traffic pattern of the floor, and students frequently reported that they had no opportunity to meet with even their closest neighbors.

"Certainly loneliness, isolation, and social awkwardness are not ordinarily strangers to people of college age. However, it was my impression that the Columbia experience fostered rather than ameliorated such experiences. Firstly, the dormitories were constructed without sufficient care given to the social needs of students. Secondly, those who should be the representatives of adult society, introducing young men to experiences with male authority that would augment, correct, or alter earlier concepts brought from home or through readings and experience with the wider culture were simply not available. It is by now cliché (but nonetheless true) to point out that most of the men to whom the students turned in admiration were simply too busy with their own academic careers to devote much energy or attention to talking with students. At the Counseling Service it was often poignant to hear of the difficulties encountered by young men desperately in need of a male model who would wait on line for a few minutes of a professor's time during one of his two office hours in a given week. There are, of course, notable exceptions; men who were able to maintain their academic productivity and also be available for social relationships with students. . . . However, these men were and are few and far between."

In the case of undergraduates, the inferior quality of student life outside the classroom frequently appears to have been accompanied by a feeling of second-class citizenship in the classroom. Columbia is one of the very few universities where graduate students outnumber undergraduates. We are aware of Columbia's justified pride in the extraordinarily high level of instruction offered undergraduates, but the emphasis she has chosen to place upon graduate work, plus the sheer weight of numbers, leaves many undergraduates with a sense of neglect on the part of both the University and many professors. Furthermore, the relatively small size of the college at Columbia leaves the University without as large a center of gravity as other universities, to provide common institutional loyalty and coherence.

Such conditions are not wholly remediable in a large urban center without enormous expenditures of money and devotion. Even then it is unlikely that Columbia could or would wish to emulate the residential colleges and houses of Harvard and Yale, or to seek to make the university the center of all its students' activities as in small towns dominated by an academic community. Yet the quality of student life at Columbia is surely not beyond human influence and the failure to improve it must be put down as one of the causes of the April uprising.

B. *Faculty Detachment*

Columbia inherited from the days of Nicholas Murray Butler, if not earlier, a strong tradition of executive responsibility. President Butler made autocratic decisions, consulting the Trustees, important alumni and donors, and City officials when he felt it advisable, but otherwise acting by himself. The important point is that the faculty did not participate. It was left free for scholarship and instruction. There was extraordinarily high intellectual kinship and morale but little encouragement of a strong sense of institutional responsibility.

During the later years of President Butler's tenure, a vacuum of power began to develop which, to some degree, continued into the 1960's. Strong local autonomy developed in many areas as the deans of the various professional schools and the departmental chairmen in the University proper assumed independent power in matters affecting their separate units. The importance of this development is illustrated by comparison of the new and well-equipped professional school buildings with the old and inadequate structures housing the College and Graduate Faculties. Indeed, the present $200 million capital fund drive has as one of its implicit purposes the re-establishment of a more equitable balance.

But the development of separate baronies left the same central deficiency: the faculty did not participate in institutional decisions and, therefore, could contribute little to provide the University with internal coherence. About a year ago, the Administration gave evidence of its desire to begin to evolve a system of greater participation, but no actual changes were accomplished.

This inherited style is reinforced by the formal structure of Columbia University. There is no university senate or similar body to represent the faculties as a whole. No single unified and dominant faculty of arts and sciences exists to serve as the University's heart. Instead of a faculty of arts and sciences, there are three separate faculties: Political Science, Philosophy, and Pure Science, as well as the partially overlapping Faculty of Columbia College. The University Council is a small body that concerns itself principally with formal programs of study and the requirements for higher degrees. The Advisory Committee of the Faculties is drawn from Committees on Instruction of the individual faculties, but size and tradition disable it from serving as a forum for developing broad educational policy.

Columbia's organization and style of administration appear to have had a number of unhappy consequences that rendered the University more vulnerable than it might otherwise have been to the risks of student uprising.

First, they created a wide and unbridged gulf between the faculty and the Administration (i.e., President, Vice-Presidents and Deans). That the faculty and the Administration should be conceived to have disparate interests—that there should be need for a *tripartite* committee on discipline representing students, faculty, and the Administration, for example—strikes the outsider as both evidence and source of internal weakness. The extent of the gulf between the Administration and the most active members of the faculty became apparent to all during and following the April disturbances.

Second, the faculty became more and more remote from problems of student life and general university policy not directly related to formal instruction. The authoritarian manner, on one side, and aloofness, on the other, were mutually reinforcing. We were told that broad university problems or policies were hardly ever subjected to thorough discussion in faculty meetings. Reports of faculty committees were usually made to the President without general faculty distribution; the Administration then took such action as it deemed appropriate without further consultation. This is not to say that the faculty lacked power if it chose to put its hand on the levers. But its older members preferred individual autonomy to collective responsibility, and the junior members had little influence. The faculty as a body and most of its members as individuals failed to speak out upon matters of intense student concern. The sudden involvement of members of the Ad Hoc Faculty Group during the April disturbances, as well as the subsequent flurry of organizations interested in restructuring the university, gives the most dramatic evidence of their earlier detachment.

Third, the faculty's lack of concern for the non-curricular interests and needs of students was all too evident to students themselves. We are not unmindful of the pressures of modern scholarship upon the individual professor, especially when joined with government or private consulting. Yet the scale of priorities at Columbia all too regularly put the students' problems at the bottom. Despite notable individual exceptions, there was little friendly and informal discussion between student and teacher about matters of institutional concern. If the faculty member could not explain university policies to worried students, perhaps it was because he did not know enough about them to explain them to himself. We are persuaded that the faculty's remoteness from the worries and grievances of students and its lack of vigilance *vis-à-vis* the Administration were significant factors in the development of an atmosphere in which student unrest could reach the point of combustion.

Fourth, there is considerable evidence that the central administration was not equipped by staff or organization to supply the central core necessary to provide institutional character and coherence strong enough to withstand divisive forces in a period of emotional tension. The total inadequacy of the counseling service is one illustration of the lack of adequate numbers concerned with student life. Further evidence is found in the constant improvisation to which the Administration was driven in dealing with student problems, including demonstrations. The governance of the tens of thousands of people who compose Columbia University requires systemization through uniform rules and established organs and agencies. In their absence, arbitrary power flourishes. Power, in turn, encourages recourse to improvisation under pressure. Columbia University gives ample evidence of this malady. The importance of *ad hoc* instruments created during student disturbances is itself convincing evidence of this unhappy condition.

Finally, although we do not assign it any great importance, we are concerned by the lack of communication and understanding between the faculty and trustees. The development of formal or informal institutions like the Harvard Visiting Committees, bringing the trustees and interested alumni into much closer contact with the several faculties and departments, as well as the problems of student life, would go far to build the mutual confidence that was evidently lacking during the April crisis.

C. Community Relations

The civil rights movement furnishes the background against which one must view Columbia's relations with the surrounding community, in both issues and student reaction. The record before us is filled with the strongest criticism of Columbia's conduct in relation to its non-institutional neighbors both in Harlem and on Morningside Heights. The criticism comes from faculty, students, political figures, and neighborhood organizations. Their testimony is confirmed by our inquiries in knowledgeable circles.

One criticism stresses the indifference of Columbia to the most pressing problems of her poorer neighbors. The charge is that she has not only failed to help and displayed no interest, but sometimes has rather arrogantly indicated that the problems of the poverty-stricken minorities surrounding her could be of no active concern to an intellectual community. When forced into contact with Harlem, as in the case of the projected gymnasium in Morningside Park, Columbia—in the eyes of the critics—appeared guilty of patronizing hypocrisy, concealing a selfish acquisition, rather than cooperative with self-respecting and equal members of the same community. Thus, the Columbia publication *Partners in the Park* made more enemies than friends among Columbia's neighbors. After minorities and other depressed groups had moved into Morningside Heights, the criticism runs, the University bent its efforts to restoring the area as an upper-middle class community. In this connection, we were referred to absence of University efforts to bring its expertise to bear on community problems, specifically to the University's unwillingness to use its resources in medicine, psychology, and the social sciences, to rehabilitate the prostitutes, drug addicts, and other derelicts in SRO * buildings, instead of buying them in an effort to "clean up" the vicinity.

Another group of criticisms concerns the manner in which Columbia has pushed her physical expansion. That the University must grow is obvious; that any expansion in this crowded urban area is bound to create friction between Columbia and her neighbors is beyond rational dispute. The critics acknowledge these facts, but charge that University officials have erred in at least five respects.

1. It is alleged that wholly unnecessary units are being brought into the vicinity. The acquisition of land for the School of Pharmacy and the new facility of the National Aeronautics and Space Administration are cited as examples.

2. Columbia is criticized for lack of planning, or unwillingness to reveal long-range plans. On many occasions University spokesmen refused to disclose the University's intentions. A number of spokesmen made public, condescending remarks as to the irrelevance of community needs when placed in opposition to those of Columbia. On at least one occasion Columbia is said to have violated an agreement with the City concerning future acquisitions. In 1965, the then Borough President, Constance Motley, held a series of meetings after which each institution on Morningside Heights marked on a map the areas into which expansion was intended. The Board of Estimate on

---

* SRO has become the symbol for single room occupancy—a type of tenancy that attracts many single, elderly people and some students as well as the kinds of occupants mentioned above.

April 22, 1965, adopted a resolution stating that it was the sense
of the Board:

> That there be no expansion on Morningside Heights of
> Columbia University or any other existing institutions,
> within the next ten years, other than the proposed expansion
> plan shown on the map . . .

Within four months, according to the testimony, Columbia
bought an SRO building at 542 West 112th Street and
turned it over to the National Aeronautics and Space Administration. A witness familiar with the area testified that, "Since
then, I would say Columbia has purchased maybe some 15
or 20 buildings not shown on this map, and has put them to
institutional use." Such incidents, like inconsistent and contradictory statements to community leaders, are said to have
bred an atmosphere of extreme distrust.*

3. Columbia is charged with unduly harassing tenants in
order to evict them, and with icy indifference to the problems
of relocation. One incident is worth recalling. In 1962 or 1963,
the then Vice-President Lawrence Chamberlain announced
that the University was opening an office of neighborhood
services that would help the tenants relocate when Columbia
took over a building. In 1963, the College of Pharmacy acquired buildings and began to evict the tenants in order that
it might move from 68th Street to the Heights. The tenants
were given no assistance in resettlement. The College of
Pharmacy, when questioned, explained that, although widely-
known as part of the Columbia complex, it was not bound by
the announced policy because technically it was a distinct
entity with only Columbia affiliations.†

---

* The incident strikes us as an excellent example of spiralling
misunderstanding arising from distrust. The map presented tentative expansion plans only, which was duly noted at three places on
its face. Nevertheless, Columbia's later acts made the entire exercise seem gratuitous, and therefore even more irritating to the
community.

† Ironically, the College of Pharmacy was unable to raise
sufficient funds for its new building and did not move to the
Heights.

4. There was criticism of Columbia's failure to plan for an integrated community of multi-purpose buildings with a full variety of people from every social and economic stratum. As the critics saw it, the University was guilty of two faults: first, it acquired the land it needed and devoted it solely to institutional purposes without consideration of the needs of the community or the values of multi-purpose buildings from which everyone might benefit; second, it sought quite ruthlessly to drive out those at the bottom of the economic ladder upon the ground that they included too many criminals, drug addicts, and other social misfits.

5. There was virtually unanimous agreement among the witnesses that Columbia failed to make any serious effort at genuine cooperation with community leaders in reconciling the necessity for expansion with the wishes of her neighbors. The image created by University officials, as the witnesses described it, is exemplified by a Columbia publication describing the effort "to cleanse and restore" Morningside Heights:

> . . . Self-styled political leaders and other quarrelsome elements, often finding allies among professional politicians, have done much to impede the renewal plan.
>
> But Morningside Heights has been cleaned up anyway, and is now one of the safer parts of the city. All but two of the worst SRO houses have been eliminated, and nobody really regrets their passing.

The Fact-Finding Commission could not dig deeply into the merits of the foregoing criticisms of the University's policies in the acquisition and use of real estate. Such an inquiry would have required time and facilities far beyond our means. We recognize, moreover, that the necessity of expansion brought unavoidable conflicts and criticism; within seven or eight years, according to one witness, the institutions on the Heights acquired over 150 buildings and displaced some 7,500 persons. The very nature of our assignment probably produced a disproportionate number of critical witnesses, both because the April disturbances required justification and because critics are usually more alert to a forum than friends. Nevertheless, after all allowances for these factors, we remain greatly impressed by the extent and sincerity of the criticism and the wide variety of sources from which it came. We were also shocked by a far wider, if less knowledgeable, feeling of utter distrust in many segments of the community that lends credence to countless hostile rumors which hurt Columbia even though false. Columbia cannot flourish in upper Manhattan until it establishes a new and sounder relation with its present neighbors.

Much of the difficulty appears to be traceable to the conflict between, on the one hand, the older commercial philosophy that the acquisition of land is purely a matter of financial power in the market place and, on the other hand, the newer emphasis upon community renewal, egalitarianism, and social cooperation. The two are not easily blended, and we cannot predict the ultimate accommodation. But Columbia's policymakers pursued the older philosophy too exclusively and long after it ceased to be viable. The approach exemplified in the publication quoted above is not only socially and morally wrong—which is enough to condemn it; it is also unworkable in the social and political climate of 1968 because it is unacceptable to too large a proportion of both the University family and its neighbors. The University cannot prosper spiritually or intellectually as an isolated island surrounded by distrust.[*]

Columbia's unhealthy relations with her neighbors had a threefold connection with the April disturbances. First, one of the immediate student demands was for the abandonment of a projected new gymnasium which symbolized the policies that neighborhood activists and many radical and liberal members of the University's own family deemed wrong.[†] Second,

---

[*] We fear that this is the inevitable consequence of continuing to issue statements with the overtones of the following sentence:

> Although the hostility of the Morningside Heights groups is inevitable and understandable it is nevertheless unjustified because there is no other alternative [to university expansion].

See: *Alumni Recommendations for the Future Government and Operation of Columbia University*, August 12, 1968.

[†] See pp. 76–89.

in a crisis it cost the Trustees and Administration support they badly needed. Third, the criticisms and distrust of the University's attitude toward the surrounding community were of a piece with the dissatisfaction among her students. Both arose out of the feeling that University officials were indifferent to the views of those most affected by its decisions. In both cases some form of meaningful participation is essential.

D. *Morale*

The cement that binds a diverse university together has important components of participation and institutional pride. Although our conclusion is not demonstrable by either fact or logic, we have the strong impression that the Columbia of April 1968 was vulnerable to the tearing forces of social upheaval because there was denial of participation, and because self-confidence had yielded to a latent feeling of malaise which the tension of the April disturbances raised to the level of frustration, resentment, and distrust.

This section of our report describes some of the evidence and sources of the loss of institutional confidence. Taken by themselves they give a distorted picture of Columbia University and its Administration yet they had profound influence upon the institution and the outward course of events.

Faculty resignations. Since September 1965, much attention has been focused upon the number of men leaving the Columbia faculty. Departures seemingly took a severe toll in the departments of history, economics, and public law and government. The explanations are undoubtedly diverse—competition and "labor mobility" are affecting academe—but a number of those leaving were openly upset over the institutional conditions under which they had to work. A senior physics professor was "sharply critical of the university's lack of consultation with academic personnel in planning its new facilities." Another senior professor, also in the physical sciences, cited inadequate laboratory and research facilities as a particular cause for his resignation. In the natural sciences, the zoology department was especially hurt, and the then-Dean David B. Truman remarked that a new life sciences building was badly needed. *Spectator,* the daily newspaper of Columbia College, interviewed many of the departing professors. The responses, published in February 1966, included charges of aimless drift.

It would require a deeper study than ours to determine whether the number of resignations has been unusually large and, if so, whether the causes are correctible. The important fact, for present purposes, is that many faculty members and students became convinced that the number of faculty departures was both significant and increasing.

Faculty salaries. Since the mid-1960's the relative salaries of Columbia's faculty members have pretty steadily declined. The well publicized American Association of University Professors annual salary rankings for all full-time teachers showed Columbia in the following national position:

1963–64	5th	place
1964–65	9th	"
1965–66	15th	"
1966–67	12th	"
1967–68	17th	"

We do not suggest that salaries are a measure of morale in an academic community. Many of Columbia's teachers, in all ranks, are unshakably dedicated to the institution. Yet comparative salary trends do affect morale and, in conjunction with other factors, often indicate where an institution is headed.

Faculty housing. Housing is a more severe problem at Columbia than any comparable institution. Since the difficulties are inherent in her geographic location, inadequate housing will always be a source of difficulty for the University and of complaint from its teachers. Happily there will also be many who feel that the disadvantages are far outweighed by the advantages of life in the world's most exciting metropolis.

From our standpoint the housing problem has two significant aspects. More than 50 percent of Columbia's staff at or above the rank of assistant professor live outside Manhattan. More than 40 percent live outside New York City. The dispersion tends to make Columbia a 9 A.M. to 6 P.M. institution. It diminishes the dialogue upon University issues within the faculty and among faculty and students. It makes it harder to give a sense of community and improve the quality of student life.

Early in 1966, a Committee on Faculty Housing, under the chairmanship of Professor Rufus W. Mathewson, Jr., was established under the Advisory Committee of the Faculties. The Mathewson Committee submitted its findings to the President in June 1966. The report dealt, in great measure, with the problem of low faculty morale, caused by housing problems in the Morningside Heights area and made worse by the "secrecy, discourtesy and arbitrariness which characterized the operations" of the University Housing Office.

The report was never made public. We are told that initially a delay in publication was the result of difficulties in communication caused by personnel changes, and that by the time the oversight was discovered much of the material was outdated. We do not question the explanation; but this was not the only controversial report never to go beyond the Administration.* Non-disclosure of matters of general faculty or student concern is, at best, a source of irritation and, in times of strain, a cause of cynicism and distrust. The treatment of the housing report was no exception. We are glad to note that Dr. Truman agreed that there should be a regular procedure for distributing all such reports to the faculty.†

Graduate education. Two incidents affecting Columbia's graduate program adversely affected the University's morale.

In mid-1966, a national survey of graduate studies by the American Council of Education was published. It detailed a significant and widespread decline at Columbia in all areas of study—physical and natural sciences, social sciences, and the humanities—between 1957 and 1966. Where Columbia had theretofore consistently ranked among the first three universities in the country, the current ranking of individual

---

* See pp. 49–51.

† Dr. Truman also testified that, although the Mathewson Report was not released, many of its substantive recommendations were put into effect, such as reorganization of the Housing Office, the establishment of a priority system of assignment, and the institution of negotiations for preparation of a master plan for the University's development on Morningside Heights.

departments dropped uniformly below fifth place, and not
infrequently, below tenth. Some aspects of the survey were
puzzling, as where the caliber of the professional staff was
ranked higher than the departments in which it taught.*
Nevertheless, a faculty as conscious of its status as Columbia's
could not overlook so critical a report.

In April 1967, the Ford Foundation omitted Columbia from
a $41.5 million grant to ten major universities for the restruc-
turing of doctoral programs. McGeorge Bundy, President of
the Ford Foundation, criticized the University's tradition of
graduate education which forced students to work part-time
while in pursuit of their degree; he stated that Columbia lacked
the motivation for reform.

Many of the faculty were both surprised and upset. Dean
Ralph Halford and Vice-Dean Herbert Deane of the Columbia
Graduate Faculties expressed the opinion that the University
had moved far ahead of its peers through the establishment of
a four-to-five-year Faculty Fellows Program which provided
"cradle-to-grave" financial support for doctoral students.† We
hope that they are correct. Yet the vote of "no confidence" had
a further demoralizing effect on the faculty and student body.

Class ranking. Under the policy of the Selective Service
System prevailing in 1965, a student's class standing was
widely, and sometimes correctly, believed to be a determining
factor in draft classification, with the low-ranked losing their
student deferments. Many colleges and universities, including
Columbia, supplied class rankings to local Selective Service
Boards.

The practice aroused wide discussion and became a log-
ical object of student protest. If the war and the draft were
evil, as many students believed, furnishing class rankings
made the university and the individual professor guilty accom-
plices because this was a form of active cooperation. Many
professors were troubled by the academic consequences of

---

* In some instances the explanation is in the physical facilities,
variety of programs, etc.

† The academic responsibilities of the fellows, the size of the
program and the adequacy of funds have recently come under
serious question.

making grades literally matters of life or death, and teachers into the vehicles of conscription. In recent years, moreover, all student grades have aroused considerable controversy, partly because of a wish to relax the pressures of student life and partly because the tide of egalitarianism has even affected intellectual judgments. The questions are both subtle and complex. Student and faculty opinion over the country was far from unanimous, but the demand for withholding class rankings furnished a rallying point for those desiring the intellectual community to take meaningful action expressing its opposition to the war.

At Columbia, the Independent Committee on Vietnam organized a student movement for a binding referendum on the distribution of class rankings by the University. The Columbia University Student Council (CUSC) scheduled a referendum for the third week in February 1966. Late in January, the Faculty of Columbia College voted, by an overwhelming majority, to request the Administration to withhold class standings from local Selective Service Boards. In the February referendum Columbia College students voted 2½ to 1 to ask the University not to release class ranks. The undergraduate body as a whole—the College, Barnard, School of Engineering, and School of General Studies—voted against the release of class ranks by 4 to 1. Shortly later, a number of student organizations planned a one or two day student strike to support the referendum.

On March 9, 1967, President Kirk announced a convocation of the University Council to consider the question. The student strike was postponed. The Council, on March 24, voted unanimously to withhold class rankings from the Selective Service Boards, while 500 to 600 students stood silent vigil on the steps of Low Library.

The Board of Trustees, at the April meeting, voted to abolish the computation of class standing altogether upon purely educational grounds.

The development and resolution of this issue had a number of significant aspects. A national issue—government policy in Vietnam—was brought to the campus; and the University, by whatever form of words it used, was induced to take action.

Thereafter it would be all the more natural for students frustrated by their inability to influence national policy to turn on the University as a surrogate. The students by-passed established channels; this was the first time in many years that there had been serious talk of the students striking. On the other hand, it was equally significant that the processes by which academic communities must form a consensus had worked out a result essentially satisfactory to everyone concerned.

Yet the upshot did not wholly quiet concern about the Trustees' decision to substitute a total abolition of rankings for the College Faculty's vote to withhold them from the draft boards. The substance of the decision was readily defensible. There are very strong academic reasons for eliminating class rankings. Other academic institutions have abolished them without the faintest thought of their bearing upon the draft. To act, or even seem to act, upon academic issues for political reasons raises subtle yet vital questions for a university with which the Board of Trustees might be properly concerned. But the fact remained that the Board, probably on the recommendation of the President, took substantially different action than the students requested and the Faculty of Columbia College and the University Council recommended. Furthermore, by announcing that the grounds of their decision were purely educational, the Trustees seemed to be overruling both the College Faculty and the University Council, without consultation, in a realm in which the faculty might claim the greater competence. And President Kirk was quoted as saying that the action of the student body "had not influenced the Council's decision."

Standing alone, the matter would be too trifling for mention. It is important because it was one of an unfortunate number of occasions on which University officials conveyed an authoritian impression and the benefits flowing from a constructive step were diminished by the manner in which it was stated.

Strawberries and the IDA. Two other little incidents that have been distorted and magnified out of all proportion nonetheless reveal a style of administration that cumulatively built resentment among faculty and especially students seeking some kind of effective voice in decisions of vital concern to them.

During the early part of 1967, as a result of the disclosure of secret subsidies by the Central Intelligence Agency, the attention of many university campuses was focused upon "secret research." At Columbia SDS became especially interested in the Institute for Defense Analyses. We recount the story later because Columbia's affiliation with IDA became an issue in the April disturbance.* Here, it is enough to say that SDS researchers had learned about the affiliation—it was a matter of public record in published reports—sometime before Dean Ralph Halford appeared at a faculty smoker to discuss the University's contracts for government research. At that time it was not widely known that Columbia was an institutional sponsor of IDA. An SDS researcher asked Dean Halford some form of question about a connection between Columbia and IDA and received an answer which he took as a denial of any connection. Shortly later, SDS charged that Dean Halford had lied in an effort to conceal Columbia's complicity. Dean Halford was thinking of the University's research contracts, but, quite possibly, he used words at the smoker which others, thinking of the IDA affiliation, would understand to be a much broader denial than the Dean intended.† We see not the slightest reason to question Dean Halford's sincerity.

---

* See pp. 89–95.
† Dean Halford testified:

I understood him to be asking: Did the University have any obligations to perform any services for the Institute for Defense Analyses.

I categorically denied that we did. There were no contracts in existence. Any members of the University who performed services for the Institute did it as private individuals, as consultants.

I was thoroughly aware of the fact that the University held membership in the corporation and, also, to my mind the obligations of that membership were so minimal, in an op-

Later, while he was being asked about the denial, Dean
Halford was quoted as using words to the effect that such
matters as the IDA affiliation were "not in the purview of
faculty and students. . . . This is a matter for the Trustees
of the University to decide." The Dean testified:

> I was attempting to convey to Professor Lang that, in the
> absence of an obligation to perform services, such as a
> contract between IDA and the University, where they
> could have some control, at least in a formal, legal sense,
> over the actions or requirements of actions by individuals
> in the University, that these matters were simply not in the
> purview of my office, nor generally were such matters in
> the purview of the faculty or the student body. By that I
> did not mean they were excluded from them by any policy,
> but just simply, heavens, there must be thousands of
> things that are done here and there around the University
> which are not publicly announced, and criticism or even
> comment invited about them.

There was no widespread reaction to these incidents on
the campus but, then and later, they contributed strong evidence of official indifference to student feelings. When interpreted uncharitably and put in juxtaposition, the two incidents
also furnished effective weapons for spreading distrust for the
integrity of the University in dealing with students.

A few months after the IDA incident, *Spectator* published
an interview with Herbert Deane, the Vice-Dean of the
Graduate Faculties, that attracted a good deal more attention.
He was said to have asserted that a consensus of students and
faculty should not, in itself, have any influence on the formation of administrative policy: "A university is definitely not a
democratic institution. When decisions begin to be made

---

erational viewpoint, that I did not take the time to try to
elaborate on them, as I recall the occasion.

There may be a question of the exact accuracy of Dean Halford's statement as applied to Electronics Research Laboratory *if*
ERL is to be treated as part of the University during that period.

democratically around here, I will not be here any longer." On the importance of student opinion to the Administration, he stated "whether students vote 'yes' or 'no' on an issue is like telling me they like strawberries." *

Vice-Dean Deane was widely regarded as a spokesman for the Administration whose statements could be regarded as accurately revealing its basic attitude toward student opinion.

Report of Committee on Student Life. In the spring of 1965, a disorderly demonstration against the Naval Reserve Officers Training Corps made it necessary to summon a contingent of New York City Police in order to restore order on the campus. In consequence, President Grayson Kirk took the constructive step of appointing a committee, drawn equally from students, faculty, and administration to conduct a "reexamination of existing university policies governing students rights and responsibilities." The Committee was chaired by Professor Aaron W. Warner. Dr. David B. Truman, then the Dean of Columbia College and Vice-President since the summer of 1967, was one of the members.

The Committee's Report and the dissenting statement of four of the five student members were submitted to President Kirk in August 1967. Both are documents of great potential significance in the future development of Columbia but, because of the way in which the Report was handled, only two aspects are significant in relation to the causes of the April disturbances.

Both documents showed sensitivity to the importance of student participation in the governance of the University, although the dissenting students were much more categorical and evidenced concern over caveats expressed in the Committee report. In the area of disciplinary procedure, for example, there was substantial agreement upon giving students a voice in the judicial function.

The Committee dealt, among other things, with the problem of indoor demonstrations. This was an issue of obvious importance to political activists in the student body. The Ad-

---

* A short time later, Dr. Deane wrote that his remarks were "elliptically reported" by *Spectator.*

ministration was greatly concerned because the indoor demonstrations in 1966 and 1967, upon issues as to which students
were sharply divided, had verged on physical violence and
endangered the safety of students. Everyone realized the
sensitivity of any restriction in areas closely related to freedom
of expression. Great care was devoted to working out a set of
rules permitting indoor demonstrations but detailing the specific regulations necessary to preserve order and safety. On
this part of the Report, the Committee was unanimous.

The Report, as we have said, was submitted to President
Kirk in August 1967. On September 25, 1967, there issued from
President Kirk's office a statement of policy that included the
rule:

> Picketing or indoor demonstrations may not be conducted
> within any University building

No explanation accompanied the announcement. The Committee which had worked long and hard in developing a less
restrictive rule was in no way consulted. Only the members
of the Committee could be aware of the extent to which their
recommendation was overridden or forgotten, but anyone interested could see that a rule of great concern to students had
been issued without participation by the faculty or themselves.

The Committee Report was not released by the President
until seven months later. In March, President Kirk wrote to
CUSC that the press of university business had prevented him
from preparing suitable comments. CUSC, having already
pressed for several months for the release of the Reports, then
made it plain that it would release the documents if the President did not. The President finally released the documents a
week before the occupation of the campus buildings.

It would be a mistake to suppose that the Report of the
Committee on Student Life was itself a major issue on the
campus. The efforts of the Council ran parallel to, but attracted
far less attention than, the gradual politicization of the campus
community. Yet, the way the report was treated conveyed an
authoritarian style and unmistakable message. The resent-
ments and frustrations they generated not only sparked the
radicals but go far to explain why so many more moderate

students joined in or supported even April's extreme demonstration.*

Tuition increases and method of payment. Witnesses from the Columbia University Student Council were sharply critical of changes in the charges to graduate students, a 1967 general tuition increase, and a sudden change in policy with respect to the deferral of tuition payments.

The change from a point system basing graduate charges upon course enrollment to flat rates for half and full-time extended study, whether wise or ill-advised, was sufficiently within the zone of University discretion.

General increases in tuition, even though they impose hardships, are inevitable at privately-endowed universities under current economic conditions. Dr. Truman's testimony fully answered most of CUSC's criticisms of the manner in which the Administration handled the increase. Although some of CUSC's inquiries might have been handled by the Administration in a warmer spirit of cooperation, it is equally plain to the observer that some of CUSC's letters were written not to join in facing a problem but with emphasis on political effect. This is an instance of the unhappy tendency of bad communications to make themselves worse; students, convinced that they are not being fairly heard on important questions, couch their views on those questions in terms that apply pressure instead

---

* We have been struck not only by the frequency with which reports of faculty as well as student committees are ignored or overridden but also by the absence of any regular procedure for distribution. In this regard the experience of the 24-member President's Advisory Council on Urban Minority Affairs, appointed to plan for the utilization of a $10,000,000 Ford Foundation grant, is revealing. In May 1967, the three student members resigned, charging the body was a "sham"; that the Council "met only three times in five months; that no votes were taken, no decisions reached, no subcommittees established, no advising done." At the same time one faculty member disassociated himself from the panel for similar reasons. Decisions were taken by a five-man Executive Committee. Eventually, the Executive Committee reported to President Kirk. Its report was discussed with several concerned groups, but it did not receive general circulation.

of reason, and their tone, in turn, discourages sympathetic administrative response.

The handling of tuition deferrals, however, is an example of the administrative style that aroused student unrest. Until the end of the academic year 1965–1966, Columbia had been extraordinarily lenient about letting students defer paying a semester's charges until the beginning of the next semester or even later, virtually without interest. About 80 percent of the students took advantage of the practice. In the summer of 1966, the University mailed out letters stating that it would no longer carry the deferred payments but had arranged for Educational Funds, Inc., to provide a tuition deferment plan. EFI charged 4.5 percent interest and scheduled inflexible monthly payments. Columbia's seal appeared on the EFI brochure.

The change is readily understandable as a necessary step in tidying up an excessively casual method of handling finance. The University had slipped into carrying several hundred thousand dollars in deferred payments it never really intended. But the suddenness of the step unnecessarily increased the resulting irritation. The action was taken without discussion with the deans of financial aid, the faculty, or members of the student body. Many students claimed never to have received the summer letter. In October 1966, when CUSC President David E. Langsam wrote President Kirk a letter asking nine questions regarding the absence of consultation with students and faculty, the relationship of EFI to Columbia, and the comparative costs of the two plans to the University, the President answered only two of the nine.

The Strickman Filter. Columbia's pride and confidence in the management of her affairs were seriously shaken by entanglement in the controversy over the Strickman cigarette filter. Robert Strickman, an inventor who asserted the invention of a filter that would greatly reduce the risk of cancer in smoking cigarettes, offered to assign control to Columbia with a division of the profits. The Board of Trustees, hearing little professional opposition from the Medical School, apparently treated the matter as a business arrangement of overwhelming potential. Leaks to the press and stock market speculation forced a premature announcement at a time when many questions concerning the composition and effectiveness of the filter, the form of University sponsorship, and the expected monetary proceeds could not be answered. The controversy became progressively more embarrasing. Many of the faculty criticized an educational institution's entering into a strictly business arrangement. Others charged insufficient testing. President Kirk's uninformed testimony before the Senate Commerce Committee made the case look even weaker. Later a split developed between Mr. Strickman and the University. The incident, which spanned eight months, was a profound embarrassment to the name and reputation of Columbia.

In seeking to diagnose the conditions that led to the tearing April disturbances, we perforce emphasize the symptoms of infection. In the longer view, it is essential to maintain a different perspective. Columbia is a great university. We believe her condition to be fundamentally sound. Her strengths and values greatly outweigh the shortcomings. Nor should anyone overlook the very great contributions of the University's leaders during the time of which we write. The detail in which our diagnosis seeks to trace symptoms to their source should not be allowed to obscure our briefly-stated but deeply-felt belief in the strengths, values, and importance of the institution.

Indeed, the loss of perspective was both a cause and a consequences of the violence of the April upheaval. The exaggerations found their initial impulse chiefly in the emotional tensions of the war in Vietnam and a social upheaval that the University's leaders apparently failed to understand. They were given new impulse, as we shall see, first by the emotional stress of the initial seizure of the buildings and, later, by the trauma of massive intervention by the police. Militant student organizations on the left were active in seeking to spread and manipulate distrust, but their overall importance seems a good deal less than sometimes supposed.

V

STUDENT ORGANIZATIONS

A. *Students for a Democratic Society*

Aroused by racial injustice and conditions in the northern ghettos, frustrated by massive involvement in an Asian war, and fired by a passion to erase social and economic inequities in the United States, a significant and growing number of young people, now known as the "New Left," have turned toward "activist politics." Many learned the techniques of direct action in the civil rights movement. Although it suffers no foreign loyalties or obligations and certainly receives no foreign direction, the New Left in the United States is also deeply stirred by the cross-currents of ethical and political protest in other parts of the world. In an organizational sense the New Left is hardly a movement. In an ideological sense it is a welter of debate upon ideas and tactics. The lack of coherence, however, has not prevented rapid, if erratic, development and steady growth in size and influence. Almost every major university in the United States has been touched by the New Left and not a few have been shaken, perhaps Columbia more than any other.

Within the New Left's array of loose and overlapping groupings, the Students for a Democratic Society has become the most significant organization.

1. THE NATIONAL MOVEMENT

The Society dates its establishment from a convention held in June 1962, at Port Huron, Michigan. The initial membership was about 200 activists. Since 1962, the membership has jumped to perhaps 20,000, grouped in several hundred campus chapters.

A brief description of the SDS national group is significant because of the light it throws on the Columbia chapter. The Society is ideologically diffuse. It runs the gamut from center-left to communist to anarchist. It encompasses exponents of the tactics of direct action as well as those who prefer to work through more conventional political channels. The national organization has a highly decentralized structure barely kept together by a small, constantly traveling, underpaid staff located in Chicago. The membership strongly distrusts bureaucratic structures; it insists that each local work out its own programs. The local chapters vary widely in composition, tone, and tactics. As noted earlier, most members of SDS approach issues with high moral convictions and emotional commitment. Their sense of kinship and common purpose is strong, but no grand theory holds SDS together and none can justifiably be read into it.

Many kinds of activities have been supported or conducted by SDS. In its early, post-civil rights years, the Society undertook a series of Economic Research and Action Programs (ERAP) which pushed community organization in ghettos, both north and south. SDS members, working for almost no pay, moved into slums, analyzed outstanding problems, organized the community and pressured the established power structure into dealing with them. One of the best publicized ERAP ventures took place in Newark under the leadership of Tom Hayden, a founder and prominent spokesman of SDS.

The ERAP projects reflect the high degree of local autonomy and individual initiative typical of SDS. Under the permissive ideological net of the national, local chapters are free to adapt to local conditions, to "do their own thing." Anti-war teach-ins and sit-ins, draft-counseling, "free schools," and "resistance"

campaigns are recent tactical innovations of local groups that
have spread throughout the country. The trend has been to
more and more obstructive tactics, some of them of highly
dubious legality and morality. On the average, the members
have probably become more radical and less concerned with
the alienation of potential political allies.

One popular concept central to SDS is that of "participatory
democracy." PD, which stresses the right of an individual to
take part directly in all the decisions which affect his life,
can hardly bear the weight of today's complex society without
some modification. The rigidities of such decision-making
became apparent during the April disturbances. Nevertheless,
PD does represent both an important aspiration and a kind of
egalitarian standard by which members orient their activities.
The characteristics of the national SDS have been reflected in
the chapter at Columbia.

2. SDS AT COLUMBIA

SDS received formal recognition as an official Columbia
student activity in February 1966. Until occupation of the
buildings, almost all its efforts were directed toward issues
related to the Vietnam war: (1) the draft, (2) recruitment
policies, (3) class-ranking, (4) secret research, and (5) ties
with outside agencies. In terms of issues, the interests of Columbia's SDS were narrower than those of the national Society.
In terms of ideology or political direction, the two bodies were
quite similar. The Columbia chapter attracted a diffuse mixture
of communists (Maoist and Soviet), humanists, socialists, liberals, anarchists, and a-politicals. The members seldom agreed
upon tactics.

Within the organization one small group on the extreme
left often seemed to act as a coherent faction opposing the
leadership. Reputedly, its members belonged to the Progressive
Labor Party, which is a small, tightly disciplined Marxist organization with strong Maoist leanings. Known as PL, the
faction apparently operated by caucus and sometimes manipulated SDS in directions opposed by the elected leaders.

SDS was too small and diverse, however, for any one group to predominate.

SDS was headed by a chairman, a vice-chairman, and a small Steering Committee. Additional committees were added in the second year to deal with such questions as IDA, University expansion, University "racist policies," labor, and research. The Steering Committee met often, and called general assemblies at least weekly. Notice of meetings was widely published around campus. Anyone could go but attendance seldom exceeded 100 students. Because SDS was a recognized college activity, the meetings usually were held in a University building. The agenda was fixed by the Steering Committee and written on a blackboard, always subject to mass revision. Anyone in attendance could talk. Steering Committee proposals were debated, and often redebated. Some questions never got to the floor. Members often left in the middle of meetings. By and large, however, the Steering Committee secured approval for most of its proposals.

Estimates of solid SDS membership run from 50 to 100 at the beginning of 1968. On specific issues, however, such as the anti-Marine recruiting demonstrations and the anti-IDA petition, the organization could mobilize groups considerably larger than its active membership. Members came from all parts of the University but the leadership was young and primarily based in the College.

One outstanding feature of SDS was the tension between those who wanted to concentrate on public education and internal organization and those who stressed protest demonstrations. The older men favored the former approach, and one gets the feeling that some of the committees offered promise of genuinely constructive action along the lines of the ERAP projects of the national organization. The young members, whose influence later became ascendant, found the major appeal of SDS in the promise of confrontations with the Administration. College seniors in SDS even spoke of the "generation gap" that separated them from sophomore members.

Yet on issues other than the war the Columbia SDS proved remarkably slow and ineffective. For example, questions concerning the proposed gymnasium were not raised in SDS until early in 1968, long after CUSC and the Citizenship Council had taken strong positions in opposition. Even then there was little response from the members. The interests and background of most of its members gave SDS little in common with the ghetto communities around Columbia.

SDS organized a number of noisy disruptive demonstrations protesting recruitment on the campus and University affiliations with the military or foreign policy establishment, but the organization accomplished little. The only significant change in the policy—the abandonment of class ranking—was brought about by traditional forms of mobilizing opinion, with scant assistance from SDS. SDS' position on campus recruiting was rejected by both faculty and students. Membership— 50 to 100—remained quite small. Most observers on the campus saw the Columbia SDS of early 1968 as an unpopular, weak, and frustrated organization.

Yet its significance was greater for four related reasons. SDS provided a home for the heterogeneous student members of the New Left who were acquiring skill in manipulating propaganda and ready to exploit the tactics of direct action in efforts to disrupt the "Establishment." Second, SDS was constantly engaged in seeking opportunities to create distrust and dissatisfaction. Third, SDS conducted disruptive disturbances in 1967 and 1968 whose style always carried the potentiality of turning quite by chance into larger and more violent disturbances, yet which the Administration proved unable to handle effectively, partly because of the liberal community's ambivalent and uncritical attitude toward disruption. Fourth, SDS provided a forum for endless discussion of militant and revolutionary tactics.

One of the causes of the April disturbances was the organized effort of a tiny group of students, within SDS, whose object was to subvert and destroy the university as a corrupt pillar of an evil society. We cannot estimate the number of hard core revolutionists but we are convinced that it was tiny. Doubtless, there were many more, attracted to SDS for sundry idealistic reasons, who talked—and in April 1968 lived—revolution, half-seriously and half in a dream world. Unfortunately, the failure of both the Administration and much of the faculty (although they erred in different directions) to distinguish the former group from the great body of students genuinely concerned with improving the University not only left the University philosophically and tactically unprepared for the crisis, but also prolonged its duration.

In saying this we do not mean to imply that Columbia suffered the April uprising because of an organized conspiracy. The tiny group of revolutionists and their endless discussion of the tactics of revolution would have been utterly impotent without more substantial and pervasive underlying causes of unrest. Thus, we attribute no importance to the report that plans for a seizure of University buildings were drawn up at a caucus during a National Students Association Conference at College Park, Maryland. If such talk occurred, it was undoubtedly like the grand campaign of political action drawn up by Mark Rudd in October 1967, for halting Columbia's "complicity" in the Vietnam war.* Mr. Rudd's program was, at most, a manifesto for the vast expansion of SDS activities. Its early phases embraced little more than conventional political action to mobilize the support of the majority of the students who were already against the war. Either the plan was rejected or it proved hopelessly beyond the slender means of SDS to effectuate, for none of it was ever carried out. The coincidence that the plan put the climax in April, when the buildings were actually seized, is not enough to hide the fact that the actual seizure came by happenstance and neither then nor earlier did events follow Mr. Rudd's projected course.

The true significance of such plans, in our opinion, and also of the endless hours of SDS discussions of revolutionary tactics, is that they accustomed many reform-minded students to the idea that resort to disruption is an acceptable method of pursuing one's goals if only the goals can be called conscientious. For others, even violence came to seem acceptable. The discussions, usually within the same circle, became platforms for self-justification, especially in the vacuum created by the lack of consensus in the intellectual community regarding the acceptable limits of dissent.

* See Appendix B, pp. 205–207.

B. *The Students Afro-American Society*

SAS only recently gained prominence as an important student organization at Columbia. Founded about four years ago
as a campus discussion group under the leadership of Hilton
Clark, the organization refrained from both political activism
and traditional service society functions. Indeed, one impetus
for the establishment of SAS was to give the black students on
campus—who were fewer than 25 in number—a sense of "identity." Another—the source of the first—was the environment
of racial discrimination.

The Society became a recognized Columbia organization
during the 1964–65 academic year. Its activities consisted primarily of the publication of a journal called the *Black Student*,
which first appeared in the spring of 1966, and the organization of a black student conference in the fall of 1967. The
University was the primary source of financial assistance during the early years of SAS.

As the black students at Columbia grew in number (36
were admitted as freshmen in 1967) and widened their interests, SAS edged toward greater political involvement. They
joined with other student groups in an effort to organize the
cafeteria workers at Columbia who were primarily black and
Puerto Rican. More than a dozen students formed the nucleus
of a pledge class of Omega Psi Psi, a predominantly black
national fraternity. Nevertheless, despite the degree of unity
achieved among black students at Columbia and their concomitant stronger sense of black-ness, their political power
remained negligible. The sporadic efforts to achieve political
influence were generally ineffective at the University. We do
not here delve into the sources of political weakness but merely
note that the disturbances of April 23–30 catapulted SAS into
a leadership role it had not theretofore sought or enjoyed.
Perhaps because of constant discussion of its essential assump-
tions and strategies, SAS proved ready and able to act with a
disciplined purposefulness that had no antecedent in its past.

PART TWO

HISTORY
OF THE
DISTURBANCES

I

PRIOR DEMONSTRATIONS

Neither the issues nor forms of protest exemplified in the April 1968 uprising at Columbia were born full-grown. In 1965, there occurred the first of a series of demonstrations altogether different from traditional political activities at Columbia. In style and tone, their characteristics progressively approached the disturbance of April 1968. The Administration's varied responses to the innovative tactics left uncertainty as to the consequences of disruptive conduct, while the demonstrations intensified the issues.

A. *NROTC Award Ceremony*

In May 1965, the Naval Reserve Officers Training Corps was scheduled to hold its annual presentation of awards on Low Plaza. A group of students planned a protest which, according to rumor, would take the puerile form of disrupting the ceremony by throwing lemon meringue and custard pies. The plan went awry when rain forced the NROTC contingent and its guests to move into the Rotunda of Low Library. The protesters locked arms to form a human chain blocking the entrance. The demonstration rapidly got out of hand. The University security force was unable to restore order and a contingent of New York City Police was called onto the campus. About seven students received letters of censure.

That incident—not the April disturbances—was the first occasion of major police action, within recent memory, on Columbia's campus.

In one sense, the demonstrators' tactics were successful. In 1966, the award ceremony was held but the year-end review was cancelled at the request of the Navy. In 1967, the Administration canceled the ceremony, citing insufficient time to prepare against violence. In 1968, upon the Navy's initiative, the ceremony was permanently abandoned.

B. *CIA Recruiting: November 1966*

Columbia, like many universities, has long allowed business corporations and agencies of the national, state, and local governments to make free use of University facilities and services in their search for highly-educated employees. The practice is partly a service to Columbia students, who are individually free to meet or ignore the recruiters. Until the fighting in Vietnam stirred campus peace and anti-draft demonstrations, the practice had gone unquestioned, but as a limited form of university "cooperation" with the Armed Forces, Central Intelligence Agency, and war-related industries, it gave militant students the opportunity to raise campus issues.

The initial recruiting incident at Columbia occurred on November 15, 1966, when a CIA representative visited Dodge Hall to interview potential employees. Two hundred students, organized by SDS, marched into Dodge Hall to "ask a few questions." The CIA representative was out to lunch and did not return to campus. The following day, 150 students marched to President Kirk's office in Low Library to present a letter demanding an official statement of non-cooperation with CIA recruiters. The letter was accepted for the President, who was not on campus, by the Director of University Relations.* The students left without disorder.

* The upshot was in the best tradition of university dialogue. President Kirk met more than 500 students for a free-wheeling

C. CIA Recruiting: February 1967

When CIA interviewers returned to campus in February, 18 students blocked the doors of the rooms in Dodge Hall where interviews were scheduled. The demonstration continued until the CIA representatives announced the suspension of interviews. The demonstrators were a splinter faction of SDS, which had voted against a sit-in demonstration. Their action embarrassed the organization which eventually approved in principle, but rejected in practice, the minority's tactics.

This was the first sit-in at Columbia and, counting the interference with the NROTC ceremony two years earlier, the second physically disruptive demonstration.

The need for disciplinary measures seemed obvious, but its political aspects made the matter delicate. The Administration appointed a tripartite discipline committee made up of student, faculty, and Administration representatives to recommend appropriate action against 16 demonstrators. The procedure was novel. Under the traditional machinery, the Dean's Office would send letters to individual students informing them of University rules and requesting a mutually convenient meeting. Disciplinary action was conceived as an educational problem and usually was handled with informality and great solicitude for the student offender. Because of pressure from interested students, the new panel opened the hearings to the public and permitted legal counsel to the students.

On March 10, the President announced the action taken against the CIA demonstrators. In general, he followed the recommendations of the tripartite panel. One student, who

---

debate in the Rotunda of Low Library. Before discussion began, he read a statement which we quote in order to make the University's position on recruiting clear. "In making the facilities of the University available," he said, "the University does not undertake to make any value judgment about any of the organizations concerned. . . . Whenever the University institutionally undertakes to espouse this or that position, in a partisan situation, it jeopardizes the long-run autonomy which is the heart and soul of all University life."

already was on probation, was suspended, a stronger penalty than the panel proposed. Another student was permitted to keep a fellowship award, the revocation of which the panel had recommended.

Although the panel completed its work successfully, the procedure displeased almost everyone. SDS felt it did not go far enough because the panel's role was only recommendatory and the panel was not weighted toward student membership. President Kirk's decision to impose more severe discipline in one instance was frequently recalled a year later during the occupation of the buildings. The Administration, faced with repeated challenges to its right to sit on the committee while it was also the prosecutor, was further embarrassed by the unpleasant publicity accorded to the hearings. Nevertheless, the panel left its mark on the disciplinary procedure of the University, for when six SDS leaders were charged with disciplinary infractions one year later in an anti-IDA protest, they demanded an open hearing.

D. *Marine Recruiting: April 1967*

Two months after the Dodge Hall sit-in, a new SDS leadership called for a protest against the appearance of Marine recruiters. After gathering at the Sundial, a group of 300 SDS members and sympathizers moved into the lobby of John Jay Hall to confront the Marines. By this time SDS activities had aroused the active opposition of more conservative students, who came to be called the "jocks" because they included a high proportion of athletes. In the battle of epithets the name "pukes" attached to their opponents. Anticipating an obstructive SDS march into John Jay Hall, about 50 "jocks" had encircled the recruiting tables. Few individuals (including SDS) wanted or expected violence. Nevertheless, the lobby became jammed with students of hostile emotion. Tension mounted. There was heavy jostling and some more serious violence. Witnesses agree that it was touch-and-go whether there would be major injuries, until it was announced that the Marines would leave the campus for the remainder of the day, but would appear the next morning.

When the Marine recruiters returned, the campus became the scene of two demonstrations. About 800 anti-recruiting demonstrators picketed around Van Am Quadrangle. In opposition, approximately 500 demonstrators milled around in support of the right to free recruiting. The protest was, to a certain degree, governed by Administration representatives who helped to prevent a repetition of the preceding day's confrontation. No violence occurred; the Marines finished their work and left the campus.

The incident caused widespread reaction. The 300-man march into John Jay Hall was larger than any to precede it. The emergence of a hostile group ready to resist SDS boded trouble. Even though neither group was yet talking violence, the confrontation recalled for older men images of Communist and Nazi gangs in Germany. The danger of turbulent indoor demonstrations became obvious. Something had to be done to resolve the issue of campus recruiting.

The last point was handled effectively. In the fall the class officers of Columbia College conducted a referendum in which students were offered three choices: open recruiting, nonmilitary recruiting only, and no recruiting. Although SDS called the referendum a hoax because the results would not bind the Administration, the organization urged a vote against recruiting. When the votes were computed, 67 percent of those who responded favored open recruiting.

The same week, the College Committee on Instruction, in response to a petition by 12 faculty members, appointed a committee chaired by Professor Allan A. Silver, to consider the question of outside recruiting. Six weeks later the panel reported. It called for open recruiting on campus and, further, asked for a comprehensive study of all of Columbia's external ties. Since the College Faculty and student body had equally supported the principle of open recruiting, for a time there was general acceptance of the decision. SDS turned briefly to a more traditional approach and curtailed the use of inflammatory tactics.

The need for rules reducing the obstructionism and physical dangers attendant upon large indoor demonstrations worked out less satisfactorily. The President's Committee on Student Life addressed the issue. Its report, submitted in August 1967, contained a unanimous recommendation for the adoption of new and detailed regulations defining the permissible limits of indoor demonstrations. Dr. Truman joined in the recommendation as a member of the committee. No action was taken on this or other portions of the report. Instead, the President, on September 25, 1967, issued a statement of policy containing a blanket prohibition:

> Picketing or demonstrations may not be conducted within any University building.

There would have been controversy over the restriction under the best of circumstances. Militants everywhere are expanding their claims of freedom of speech and petition to cover increasingly turbulent and even physically obstructive demonstrations. Social tensions have created confusion over the proper limits of expression. The new rule, as stated, drew no distinctions except such as might be implied in the term "demonstrations." Students—especially Columbia students—are easily stirred by claims of interference with political liberty. SDS, upon whose tactics the new rule bore heavily, was bound to challenge it.

Whether or not the substance of the restriction was sound, the manner of its issuance and administration produced trouble. The ban was issued without contemporaneous explanation of its justification or meaning. There was no prior discussion with student organizations and no sign of consultation with the faculty. Since the members of the Committee on Student Life kept their report in confidence, there may not then have been general awareness of the fact that its unanimous recommendation had been overridden; but the controversy was still alive at the time of the April disturbances, after the committee's report was released. In the course of time, moreover, it became apparent that the meaning of the rule was far from certain. Four weeks after the rule was issued more than 300 students marched to Low Library to present President Kirk with a letter demanding the University sever its links with the military establishment. SDS, ICV and other groups participated. The groups said they would wait to see the response before deciding on further measures. The Administration responded in two ways. First, it did not answer the letter, saying that it contained no return address. Second, it decided that the march into Low Library did not constitute a violation of the ban on indoor demonstrations.

E. *Dow Chemical Recruiting: February 1968*

Although SDS was quieter during the fall semester, the scheduled visit of representatives of Dow Chemical Company on February 28, 1968, precipitated new militance. Dow, as a manufacturer of napalm, had already been the target of student demonstrations on a number of campuses. Prior to the visit an SDS general assembly voted unanimously to conduct a protest but not to obstruct the recruiters. About 12:30 P.M. over 200 SDS members and sympathizers marched to Low Library to form an orderly picket line. Suddenly, several pickets stepped out of line and moved toward Dodge Hall calling "all those who want to go meet the Dow recruiters, follow us." The picket line began to disperse. An open debate broke out on the steps of Low Library between Ted Kaptchuk, the Chairman of SDS, and those who wanted to obstruct the Dow recruiters. When Mr. Kaptchuk said, "a picket line has a purpose in its time and place," a second student yelled, "leave Ted behind." Another shouted out, "who are you going to alienate—some half-assed liberals?" Mr. Kaptchuk, sensing the mood of the more radical members in the charged atmosphere, led the group into Dodge Hall.

As the demonstrators entered the doors and stairwell of Dodge Hall, they voted overwhelmingly to stage a sit-in. Ted Kaptchuk and Ted Gold, the Vice-Chairman of SDS, conferred with University officials and the floors of the building were opened to the demonstrators. Eighty Columbia and Barnard students then staged a sit-in, causing the cancellation of seven appointments with the Dow recruiters.

No disciplinary action was taken against even those who sat-in at Dodge Hall. On the face of the words, the incident seemed to involve the plainest violation of the ban against "demonstrations . . . within any University building," but the Administration stated that the students violated no University regulations because they had neither obstructed recruiting nor picketed within a University building. A tense and potentially dangerous situation had developed at Dodge Hall. The best solution, for the immediate occasion, may well have been to let the sit-in proceed without seeking to enforce the ban on indoor demonstrations. Having gone that far to let the demonstration play itself out, the Administration could hardly turn around and impose punishment. But the retreat in the face of confrontation contained the seeds of trouble. If the march of more than 100 pickets into a building, followed by an 80-student sit-in was not a demonstration, just what was prohibited by the rule? Did the University dare enforce the rule? The more responsible members of SDS might appreciate the Administration's dilemma,* but there were others looking for

---

* One could conclude that the Administration itself created the dilemma it faced when called upon to enforce in the February 1968 indoor demonstration the ban and on the occasion of the anti-IDA demonstration that was an immediate precursor of the April disorders (see pp. 72–73). Vice-President Truman, in his testimony explaining the reason for the blanket ban, told us that the Administration had decided that a detailed regulation of indoor demonstrations striking only at their particular dangers would be impracticable. It was therefore determined that there could be no demonstrations within buildings, "and then attempt to enforce that rule in such fashion as to construe incidents that might occur as generously as possible with respect to those who were involved in the incident."

It is not clear whether this decision involved merely an understandable desire to ameliorate what was recognized as a broad and inflexible prohibition, or was a conscious determination to frame the prohibition more broadly than was needed, trusting to administrative discretion in enforcement for the sort of flexible regulation

every "angle" as they sought further confrontations. Especially the younger members found the chief appeal of SDS to be its ability to produce confrontations with the Administration. Indeed, as the internal and programmatic frustrations of SDS increased, so did its attacks on the University.

F. *The New Gymnasium: February–April 1968*

We relate below ° the full story of the controversy over Columbia's projected construction of a new multi-million dollar gymnasium in Morningside Park. In the beginning the opposition came chiefly from the neighboring community, and the demonstrations were not primarily student affairs. But since students participated and the incidents were covered in *Spectator*, they undoubtedly contributed to what one now can see as an accelerating cycle of violence in the conduct of political controversy.

On February 20, twelve people, including six Columbia students, were arrested for interfering with bulldozing by sitting-in at the site of the proposed gymnasium. Groundbreaking in Morningside Park had taken place, without ceremony, the day before. The protest was jointly sponsored by the Citizenship Council, SDS, and the Graduate Faculties Student Council.

On February 29, about 150 demonstrators marched from a Sundial rally to the gym site chanting anti-gym slogans in an attempt to prevent ongoing construction. There occurred a good deal of jostling between police and the demonstrators, several of whom attempted to pull down the fence surround-

---

that was desired. In either event, hindsight suggests the dangers of maintaining a prohibition upon student protest activity which is broader in its command than in its intended enforcement. The undeniable value of administrative flexibility may be purchased only at the overriding cost of an unclarity, which opens an administration to charges of arbitrariness on the one hand, or weakness on the other, and thus may cost it the moral support that milder and more explicit forms of regulation might enjoy.

° See pp. 76–89.

ing the site. The police were forced to call for reinforcements during the two-and-one-half hour protest and by the end of the afternoon 13 people, 12 of them students, were arrested for criminal mischief, disorderly conduct, or resisting arrest.

Early the following week, 150 Columbia students and residents of the neighborhood opposed to construction of the gymnasium forcibly entered Ferris Booth Hall to disrupt a meeting of the West Side Community Conference, an annual forum where prominent citizens meet to discuss urban problems. Shouting questions from the side of Wollman Auditorium, they harassed a number of speakers, who included Sargent Shriver, then Director of the Office of Economic Opportunity, Congressman William F. Ryan, and Roger Wilkins of the Department of Justice.

G. The IDA Demonstration: March 27, 1968

In 1967–1968, Columbia's affiliation with the Institute for Defense Analyses was the subject of heated criticism. SDS made it a subject of special attention, claiming that its researchers had exposed a link between the University and the military that University officials had tried to conceal. Because the demand for severance of all IDA affiliations was an avowed objective of the seizure of campus buildings in April, we analyze the issue at some length below.* Here, it is enough to note that on March 27, 1968, the controversy provoked another confrontation between SDS and the Administration, which proved to be the direct precursor of April's uprising.

The protest began with a noon rally at the Sundial. Mark Rudd, the newly-elected Chairman of SDS, attacked the rule against indoor demonstrations. A direct challenge was planned, but the uncertain enforcement at Dodge Hall left ample scope for questioning the Administration's interpretation. Mark Rudd's speech mocked, "If you want to yell, scream, and bust up an office, that's okay, but no demonstrating." †

---

* See pp. 89–95.

† SDS continued to make a point that the uncertainty of the

When the crowd marched to Low, it was met by members of the Administration. Associate Dean Alexander Platt told Mark Rudd that Vice-President Truman would see three of the group in his office. The offer was rejected; Mr. Rudd asked Dean Platt to meet them in the rotunda of Low Library. The demonstrators moved to the office of the Vice-President for Business, Thomas McGoey. He was handed a petition for delivery to President Kirk calling for an end of the IDA affiliation, signed by over 1,500 faculty and students. More than 100 students moved through the halls of Low Library for half an hour, carrying placards, chanting slogans and using a bullhorn.

As the demonstration broke up, Dr. Truman was seen walking across campus. The protesters briefly blocked his entry into Philosophy Hall.

On this occasion the Administration invoked the ban on indoor demonstrations. There was an immediate announcement that disciplinary action would be taken. On April 5, 1968, five college students, all SDS leaders, were summoned to Dean Platt's office to discuss their participation in the IDA demonstration. The five refused to appear unless given an open public hearing. Dean Platt refused. On April 22, 1968, the University announced that the five had been placed upon disciplinary probation. A sixth student was similarly disciplined by the Associate Dean of Graduate Faculties.

H. *The Martin Luther King Memorial Service: April 9, 1968*

On the Tuesday following the assassination of Dr. Martin Luther King, Jr., the University scheduled a memorial service in St. Paul's Chapel, conducted by the Chaplain of the University, Reverend John D. Cannon. Eleven hundred people attended. Toward the end of the service, Mark Rudd walked to the speaker's platform. Like other students his attendance was

---

rule. On April 22, when the march into Low Library that led to the occupation of campus buildings was being planned, Mark Rudd argued that, "It is difficult to tell these days which indoor demonstrations violate President Kirk's memorandum." Dean Platt acknowledged that application of the rule raised difficult questions.

welcomed, but he had no invitation to speak. In strong language he accused President Kirk and Vice-President Truman of "committing a moral outrage against Dr. King's memory" in view of the Administration's record of racism. He called the service an "obscenity." Forty people, led by SDS, then walked out of the chapel. The service continued without further disruption. At the end, the Reverend Cannon stated that any student "who feels moved by the spirit of truth, who wishes to speak his mind, is able to speak in this chapel at any time."

The incident highlights SDS' deliberate use of tactics offensive to the manners and spirit of much of the University. Of equal importance is the example it furnishes of confusion over the standards of behavior applicable to political protest. Many members of the University community were profoundly shaken. Dr. Truman, speaking about possible disciplinary action against Mr. Rudd, stated: "I don't see how this incident can be ignored." The Reverend Cannon's statement outwardly appeared to condone the deliberate offense given by Mr. Rudd, but, in fact, it was chiefly the result of prior, private conversations with other University officials which give it a different meaning.

II

THE ISSUES

April 1968 brought into juxtaposition, partly by chance and partly through skillful SDS manipulation, the three issues capable of arousing the widest and strongest student emotion:

(A) The projected gymnasium in Morningside Park, which symbolized the shortcomings of Columbia's attitude toward her black neighbors.

(B) The University's relationship to the Institute for Defense Analyses, which symbolized complicity in the war in Vietnam.

(C) The imposition of discipline upon six SDS leaders, without a formal hearing, for breach of the rule against indoor demonstrations.

The first two issues by transference focused upon the University much of the students' resentment against the political world. Both issues—and probably the third issue also—would attract wide support among political liberals and radicals within the Columbia Faculties, if not for the form the April protest took, then at least for its objectives. Since all three issues were the announced causes of the seizure and occupation of campus buildings on April 23–30, they deserve analysis in some detail.

A. The Gymnasium in Morningside Park

Development of the controversy. In 1958, when Columbia was considering its pressing need for a new gymnasium, University officials met with representatives of the Parks Department and discussed the possibility of putting it in the park. The proposed area, about two acres in size, was a rocky hillside of some beauty but little use, except for occasional children climbing over its rocks. Robert Moses, who was then Parks Commissioner, reached the basic understanding with President Kirk that, if Columbia would build a public gymnasium containing facilities for community use specified by the Parks Department, the Parks Department would permit Columbia to build a gymnasium for its own use on top of the public building.

The proposed arrangement harked back to the early 1950's when Columbia and the New York City Parks Department entered into an agreement under which the University constructed an athletic field at the southern end of Morningside Park in return for a revocable permit to use the athletic field on weekdays during the school year. The University also undertook to conduct on weekends, during the school year and throughout the summer, at its own expense, an athletic program for organized community teams. The arrangement still prevails. While some members of the community resent both Columbia's use of a park area and the rule limiting the program to organized teams, there has been no substantial, organized opposition.

The process of implementing the basic Moses-Kirk understanding by formal legislation, contracts, and leases lasted until August 1961. In May 1960, the New York State Legislature enacted enabling legislation which would permit the city, with the approval of the Board of Estimate, to lease air rights in the park to Columbia for the construction of the gymnasium. Thereafter, the proposed lease was submitted to the Board of Estimate and referred by it to various city departments for consideration. In March 1961, preliminary plans for the building were submitted by the University. The plans were approved by the Municipal Arts Commission in May of 1961.

On July 27, 1961, the Board of Estimate held a public hearing on the question whether the lease should be approved. Allen S. Burd of the Fine Arts Federation of New York, Harmon Goldstone of the Municipal Art Society, Daniel Chase of the Park Association of New York City, Inc., George Hallet, Jr. of the Citizens Union, and Dr. Lloyd Gaston of St. Luke's Hospital appeared in opposition to the proposed gymnasium. The proposal was vigorously supported by the then Parks Commissioner, Newbold Morris, and by Dr. Clarence Sherwood of Adult Youth Association, Inc., Middleton Harris of the Grand Morningside Neighborhood Group, and Mrs. James F. Murphy of the Morningside Civic Group, an organization that claimed to represent 1,600 people who lived or worked on Morningside Heights. After due consideration, the Board of Estimate approved the lease.

In August 1961, the lease was executed by Commissioner Morris and President Kirk. The executory obligations were complete.

In its final form the transaction was a lease of air rights above 2.1 acres of park land and a public gymnasium in return for Columbia's covenants to:

(1) Construct on the site, according to Parks Department plans, a gymnasium facility for public use costing the University more than $1,400,000.*

(2) Pay the expense of heating the gymnasium facility for the community and also all maintenance of the exterior of the building, at an estimated annual cost of $5,000-$10,000.

(3) Pay an additional $3,000 a year rent.

At the same time, but in an entirely separable part of the transaction, Columbia promised to conduct sports programs in the community's portion of the building at Columbia's expense.

Both Columbia and the City procured expert appraisals of the value of the air rights. The appraisers recognized that the primary consideration flowing to the City was the construction of the community portion of the gymnasium, but they deter-

───────────

* This is the ultimate figure after revision of the plans. The estimated construction cost of the original plan was about $1,000,000.

mined that in addition the University should pay a small annual cash rental. Since the rental of $3,000 a year fixed by the City's appraiser was $500 higher than the rental fixed by the appraiser employed by Columbia, that figure was chosen.

After approval of the lease the University embarked on a vigorous campaign to make the plans into reality. A $10,000,000 fund drive among alumni, friends, and other supporters of Columbia was required. The Administration and Board of Trustees, notably Harold McGuire, now Vice-Chairman of the Board, dedicated large amounts of time and effort to the enterprise in the sincere belief that the project was greatly important to Columbia. The alumni gave the project loyal support. So did many students. Thus, from 1961 to 1965 there was a vast financial and emotional commitment to the enterprise, based upon fixed legal obligations. During this period, there was no active or vocal opposition.

In mid-1965, opposition began to arise. By the spring of 1968, the opposition both in the community and among the faculty and student body was highly emotional, widespread, and deeply rooted. Contrary to statements by Columbia officials, this was—in the context of 1968—a racial issue.

The earliest post-lease expression of community opposition, so far as our record shows, was voiced in 1965 meetings of the Parks and Playgrounds Committee of the Morningside Renewal Council—an organization of civic groups established under the sponsorship of the City Housing and Redevelopment Board to represent the community in plans for urban renewal. While there was strong sentiment against the gymnasium, the members of the committee believed that the final approval of the plans made it impossible to stop the construction.

During the mayoralty campaign in the autumn of 1965, however, John Lindsay issued a White Paper on the City's parks which criticized the gymnasium project and called for reevaluation. In the view of Thomas Hoving, who headed the task force and later became Parks Commissoner, the plan offended three vital principles:

(1) The immediate neighborhood should be aroused to determine largely for itself how best to use its park lands.

(2) Open areas, being few and precious, should not be built up.

(3) Park property should not be allowed to go to private use.

The upsurge of these principles, especially the first, changed the entire social and political environment affecting the gymnasium project.

Encouraged by the White Paper and Mayor Lindsay's election, the Parks and Playgrounds Committee of the Morningside Renewal Council invited all the organizational members of the Renewal Council to send representatives to a meeting to organize opposition to the proposed gymnasium. Twenty-seven out of thirty, including seven of the nine Harlem organizations, sent representatives to the meeting early in January 1966. An Ad Hoc Committee was formed with Mrs. Amelia Betanzos, the local Democratic District Leader as chairman, and Patrick Cronan, the local Republican District Leader as vice-chairman. The Committee began to plan a protest rally in Morningside Park.

At about the same time the gymnasium came under attack from the new Parks Commissioner, Thomas Hoving. Mr. Hoving's initial statements, made in interviews published in the *World-Telegram and Sun* on December 20, 1965, and the Columbia *Spectator* on January 4, 1966, were somewhat cautious, but he did say that he "was very wary about any use of the city parks for private organizations," and that he hoped to "persuade Columbia to change the site of its proposed gymnasium."

On January 17, 1966, Mr. Hoving met with President Kirk, Harold McGuire, the Chairman of the University Gymnasium Committee, and Jackson Smith, the architect who had designed the gymnasium. At this meeting Mr. Hoving argued that there was an inequitable distribution of space between Columbia and the community—Columbia receiving 87.5 percent and the community 12.5 percent—and that the rent of $3,000 was not fair. The University representatives explained their view that the $3,000 was not the main consideration that ran to the City; in addition, Columbia would have the expense of constructing the community portion of the gymnasium and of operating the community athletic program. Although the meeting was conducted in a cordial atmosphere, it did not dissipate Commissioner Hoving's opposition. He made increasingly vigorous public statements opposing the gymnasium.

Columbia CORE came out against the gymnasium project in February 1966. In March, the Columbia University Student Council passed a resolution calling for its suspension until discussions were held with community groups. On April 24, 1966, the Ad Hoc Committee held a rally in Morningside Park, cosponsored by the West Harlem Community Organization, the Senator Basil Patterson Service Center, and the 114th Street Block Association. The Columbia University Student Council also gave active support. Although it was a rainy afternoon, approximately 120 people attended the rally. The speakers included Senator Patterson, Commissioner Hoving, and the Chaplain of the University.

The Ad Hoc Committee on Morningside Park then turned to political channels. Senator Basil Patterson and Assemblyman Percy Sutton introduced bills in the New York State Legislature to repeal the 1960 enabling legislation.

As a result of the growing opposition, a series of meetings was held during the winter of 1966 and spring of 1967 between University officials, representatives of the Ad Hoc Committee, and local political leaders including Mr. Sutton, then Borough President of Manhattan, Senator Patterson, Assemblyman Charles Rangel, J. Raymond Jones, and Mrs. Betanzos. The spokesmen for the community expressed their opposition to the proposed gymnasium and suggested that some plan should be developed by which Columbia and the community would share the entire facility. After considering these objections during an adjournment, the University officials replied that they could not agree to any sharing of the total facility but that Columbia would, at its expense, add a swimming pool to the community portion. The University spokesmen made it clear, however, that this was as far as Columbia was prepared to go. While the proposal did not satisfy the community representatives, they recognized that it was a beneficial addition. Consequently, after Mayor Lindsay indicated that the City did not have funds with which to enlarge the community

portion of the gymnasium, Borough President Sutton agreed
to sponsor a resolution in the Board of Estimate authorizing
amendment of the lease to incorporate the swimming pool.
The resolution was passed on October 25, 1967. The changes
added $400,000 more or less to the cost of Columbia and thus
to the value of the consideration received by the City. *Spectator*
quoted Borough President Sutton as saying that, although
Columbia had been delinquent in its dealings with the community, since the gymnasium's construction was inevitable,
further opposition would be "obstruction" that would simply
deny added facilities to the community.

The addition of the pool did not quiet the opposition. The
Ad Hoc Committee on Morningside Park held another meeting, at which the people from Harlem indicated that they were
tired of talking and wanted more direct action. Mrs. Betanzos
stepped aside in order to let representatives from the Harlem
area take over the leadership of the opposition. The West
Harlem Morningside Park Committee was promptly formed.
Sixteen Harlem organizations were represented on this committee. One Harlem organization, Citizens Care Committee,
favored the proposed gymnasium.

The West Harlem Morningside Park Committee met with
President Kirk, Vice-President Truman, and other University
officials on September 20, 1967. The Committee explained that
the organization had been formed by inviting all organizations
in the Harlem Morningside Heights and Manhattan Valley
areas to participate, and that the decision of these community
organizations was that the gymnasium should be fought. The
park, they said, should not be used for a private purpose. The
University officials explained the plans and the benefit to the
community. There was no meeting of minds. The members of
the Committee had been irritated by the University's bringing
to the meeting persons not connected with the Committee
whom the University introduced as representatives of the
community. They were further upset by the University's
adamant insistence upon going forward with its plans.

Thereafter, the principal activity of the West Harlem
Morningside Park group was arranging rallies and demonstrations. On July 27, 1967, there was a rally at 116th Street and

Morningside Drive attended by 80 persons. On October 24, 1967, the group sponsored a tent-in at the proposed site, in which some 50 people participated.

On December 14, 1967, the West Harlem Morningside Park Committee sponsored another meeting, attended by contrasting figures. H. Rap Brown spoke of burning down any building; Senator Patterson, a responsible and effective community representative, also spoke in opposition to the project.

On February 19, 1968, ground was broken without public announcement. The following morning approximately 20 protesters followed the work crews onto the site and blocked the construction equipment. Six students and six community residents, including Robert McKay and Joseph Monroe of the West Harlem Morningside Park Committee, were arrested. On March 2, about 150 students and community people disrupted the West Side Community Conference in order to protest the construction. In March and April, the West Harlem Morningside Park Committee sponsored three candlelight marches from 114th Street and Eighth Avenue through Morningside Heights to 116th Street and Broadway. On Saturday, April 20, Harlem CORE sponsored a rally against the gymnasium in Harlem which, according to press reports, was attended by approximately 400 people.

Although it is hard to recapture the atmosphere, there is little evidence that the gymnasium was an important campus issue prior to the April disturbances. Most people seem to have felt that it was *fait accompli*. A fair number strongly criticized the architectural design and locale. But, in the spring of 1966, after the Columbia University Student Council passed its resolution calling for suspension of further plans until discussions were held with community groups, Robert Herz, Chairman of the Student Board of Managers, had no difficulty in organizing a short campaign, even during examination week, that obtained 1,500 signatures to a statement approving the proposed gymnasium.

In 1967 and 1968, student opposition grew stronger, especially from the Citizenship Council. Students took part in the demonstration of February 20, 1968, and six were arrested. On February 28, SDS, the Citizenship Council, and the Graduate Student Council sponsored a rally in opposition during the course of which some 150 students marched to the construction site where they attempted to block the entry of a truck and tore down part of the fence. Twelve students and Reverend A. Kendal Smith, a Harlem pastor, were arrested.

On March 8, Jay Dobkin, Chairman of the Citizenship Council, proposed to Vice-Presidents Truman and Thomas McGoey and Dean Coleman that the University turn control of the entire gymnasium over to the Parks Department under an agreement that would guarantee Columbia use adequate for its reasonable needs. The arranging of schedules for the use of the gymnasium would be left to a community committee, with the City acting as arbitrator in case of disagreement between Columbia and the community group.

On March 27, 1968, the faculty of the School of Architecture unanimously adopted a resolution calling on the Trustees to reconsider the building of the gymnasium in Morningside Park.

Yet even at this point the strength of the opposition was debatable. On March 6, 1968, *Spectator* published an editorial entitled "Enough is Enough" in which it strongly supported the construction.

Appraisal. The gymnasium issue, although susceptible of easy oversimplifications, was exceedingly complex. The basic understanding was reached in 1958—seven or eight years before there was significant community opposition and almost ten years before the April uprising. In the intervening years major moral and legal commitments had been undertaken and expectations aroused on the part of students, alumni, and friends. Yet changes in the social and political atmosphere had undoubtedly moved more swiftly than events, especially in the areas of race and community relations. Whether the gymnasium was good or bad for Harlem, public property was being used for private purposes and the new spokesmen for the increasingly self-conscious black community of the mid-1960's had had no share in the planning or decisions. Once the gymnasium project became a symbol of race and community relations, it was peculiarly vulnerable because the University's relations with its poorer neighbors had badly deteriorated.

The central Administration was caught between the obligations and expectations incurred on plans approved almost a
decade earlier and the new social and political attitudes that
swept over the University before the project could be executed.

More specifically, the Commission finds that there was no
impropriety in the original project, and that the University
acted in complete good faith in negotiating an agreement with
the Parks Department which was considered fair to both the
University and the community. In this conclusion we are supported by two able Parks Commissioners of the City of New
York, Robert Moses and Newbold Morris; both strongly endorsed the proposal. Although Commissioner Hoving strongly
disagreed with the judgment of his predecessors, he testified
that his review of the Parks Department files revealed no evidence of fraud or undue influence in connection with the
negotiation of the lease.

We also find that the gymnasium project was planned and
implemented in a way that gives assurance of its fairness to
the public as a business transaction. The charge that Columbia
is guilty of over-reaching because the rent is only $3,000 is
palpably unfair. The money rent is only an insignificant part
of the benefit to the City and the cost to Columbia. The primary consideration, under the original lease, was $1,000,000
that Columbia was to spend in constructing the community
portion of the gymnasium. The addition of the swimming pool
and other changes brought this figure to over $1,400,000. The
interest on $1,400,000 of Columbia's endowment is alone equal
to an annual outlay of at least $56,000, to which must be added
the costs of heating the community gym, maintaining the exterior of the building, and operating the sports program in the
community portion of the gymnasium. Estimates of the total
outlay required to meet the latter obligations vary but apparently run from $50,000 to $80,000 a year.*

---

* There is some question whether the part of this figure attributable to the sports program can fairly be counted as part of the
benefit to the City. It was new money obligated as part of the
arrangement, but the lease specifically provides that, even if Columbia breaches its agreement to run the community sports program, that breach will not have any effect on the lease. (See
McGuire Exhibit 4, par. 28 (e).)

Both Columbia and the City of New York obtained appraisals. Both appraisers concluded that the fair rental of the community portion of the building to be constructed by Columbia for the City exceeded the fair rental value of the unimproved real estate. The $3,000 annual rent was thus an additional benefit to the City over and above an otherwise commercially equitable exchange.

Viewing the matter solely as a business transaction, there is no merit in the criticism that the community would receive the use of only 8 percent—later increased to 12 percent—while Columbia would receive 92 percent or, under the revised arrangement, 88 percent. If the University had required much less gymnasium space—for example, an area no bigger than the portion of the building dedicated to the City, the University and the City would have equal shares, but the value of what the community would receive would be exactly the same as under the actual arrangement. The community receives the same thing whether Columbia's portion is half, twice, or fifty times its size. The size of the building the University constructs for itself has little or nothing to do with the adequacy of the facilities the community receives in return for the use of the land.

We further find that the University officials were following accepted academic practices when they rejected the suggestion that the use of the entire facility be shared with the community by an allocation of time. The University was spending over $10,000,000 to construct its portion of the gymnasium. The money was raised on the understanding that it was to be used to meet the students' needs. Having made those representations and agreed to spend $1,400,000 on the community gymnasium, plus a sizeable annual outlay, in order to obtain the right to build its own gymnasium on this land, the University had the right, if not the obligation, to maintain control over its portion of the gym in order to assure its students' present and future needs would indeed be met. We know of no University willing to surrender control over major facilities used by its students.*

---

* Individual statement of Commission member Amsterdam: "I cannot agree with this paragraph. I do agree that University

Finally, on a purely pragmatic view, it would be reasonable to conclude that the community would benefit much
more from a swimming pool and gymnasium open to its young
people summer and winter, with expert guidance, than from
the 2.1 acres of rocky hillside that it lost.

But these points were not the real issue. By 1966–1968 it had
become impossible to view the arrangement simply as a business transaction—a fact which the University officials utterly
failed to grasp or, if they did indeed grasp it, utterly failed
to acknowledge. As the Chairman of the Citizenship Council
told us, the gym was "a very visible symbol of something
which is much more serious, which is the expansion program
that is going on in Columbia." Franz Leichter, a Democratic
leader in the Morningside area, articulated the same perception:

> The gymnasium is only, in my mind, a manifestation of
> that. That is, the whole uncoordinated, even legislative,
> and unchecked expansion on the Heights, and into the sur-
> rounding community. We have seen in the last seven years

---

officials were following accepted academic practices in rejecting
any split-time arrangement for the sharing of gym facilities. But
I do not think it follows that they had or have an 'obligation' to
decline to consider any form of arrangement for splitting time or
the sharing of facilities, as one possible solution to the unique and
exceedingly difficult problem of meeting community objections to
the proposed gymnasium in Morningside Park. That problem did
and still does demand imaginative, possibly innovative thinking
which need not be bound by practices generally accepted because
useful in other situations. It is true that money for the gym was
raised on the understanding that the gym would provide for the
needs of Columbia students. The understanding should be faith-
fully honored. However, it is not self-evident that every sort of
arrangement for shared facilities or split time would render the
gym unserviceable to student needs. Rather, it may be the case
that no gym can now be built, and no student needs for a gymnasium facility can now be met, unless Columbia satisfies community objections. A shared-time arrangement ought surely not
to be thought foreclosed if that develops as the most practicable
means of accommodation between the University and community."

or so some 10,000 persons displaced from Morningside Heights. We have seen over 150 buildings taken by the various institutions on the Heights, most of them by Columbia University. It is not only what was done, but also how it was done that has created the great community tension. I would say it just accelerated the antagonism of the community toward Columbia. The gymnasium, to my mind, is really only part of the feeling that the people in the area have, and I think it is justified that this large institution, which isn't subject to any of the usual pressures of society or political pressures, which is just expanding, without any limit at all, without any means of imposing any restrictions, or really without any procedures for the community to voice its opinion and to find anyone who will listen.

Thus, the nub of the issue was that the community's property was being used by a private institution, yet the newly emerging voices concerned with community action had no influence in the decision. Since the community affected was overwhelmingly black, this shortcoming symbolized all the injustices of both poverty and racism. Seen in that light and not as a practical arrangement and business transaction, the plans for a gymnasium building exemplified those injustices: Columbia would enjoy most of the building, assigning a small fraction to the people; Columbia's students would enter from the Heights but its black neighbors through the cellar. From some viewpoints these characterizations are grossly distorted; geography determined the relative positions of the University and community entrances. Yet as symbols of relative power the characterizations were not inaccurate and carried enormous weight in the political and social environment then emerging.

We think that when the extent, intensity, and responsible character of community opposition to the gymnasium became apparent—that is, by early in 1968, if not sooner—Columbia should have been more sensitive to the nature of the objections in the new social and political context, and that it should have been more open-minded toward abandonment of the gym site or radical alteration of the planned construction and use. We recognize the depth of Columbia's long-standing legal and moral commitments and the enormous difficulty of reconsidering a project to which unselfish and unsparing efforts have long been devoted. But release from such commitments may sometimes be obtained for sufficient reason, and the existence of the commitments alone did not justify Columbia's failure seriously to reconsider, in a time of changed events and attitudes, both the wisdom of the gymnasium plans and the extent of its power to secure a change if time had made the plans unwise. At the least, it was in order to give a more understanding ear to the voices of those community spokesmen who urged that reconsideration was warranted.

University officials have complained that it is impossible to know who speaks for the community because the community is not one organization but many people. We are more impressed by three opposing considerations. *First*, almost all the political leaders in the area are strongly opposed to the project. If there were overwhelming community support for the gymnasium, the political leaders would not risk the wrath of the voters by opposing it. *Second*, when the Citizenship Council wanted to try to assess community reaction to Columbia's handling of the Ford Foundation grant for the study of problems of urban minorities, its officers were able to reach some 200 community groups out of which 100 sent representatives to the campus. *Third*, today, the major spokesmen for the community include its activist leaders and organizations, who are responsibly concerned with its sound development yet are presently among the projects' severest critics.

We are also persuaded that University officials misunderstood both the nature and extent of the opposition to the gymnasium. Contrary to their assertion, the opposition was not generated by Commissioner Hoving but came from the community under the leadership of the Ad Hoc Committee. It was both genuine and constantly increasing. In the community, doubtless a poll would have shown that most residents knew little of the gymnasium and cared less. Yet all the elected officials cannot have misjudged their constituents, and the active organizations were opposed. On the Columbia campus the initial opposition, even in 1966 and 1967, was probably confined to a small group of faculty and students especially sensitive to racial issues, but as time passed, the opposition mounted. During the April disturbances 4,093 out of 6,426 students polled expressed agreement with the demonstrators' demand that construction be halted.

Even as feelings mounted, the intrinsic merits of the gymnasium project itself were never the real issue. The question then—and now—was whether there could be genuine understanding of the underlying needs and aspirations the socially conscious were seeking to express. The failure to understand them cost the University credit for agreeing to add the swimming pool because even then the Columbia officials exhibited no grasp of the nature of the opposition. Until the needs and aspirations were accepted, there was little chance the activists would be persuaded of either the essential fairness of the project or the enormous complexity of seeking to unravel an enterprise in which so much time and money had been invested. For if some members of the Columbia family opposed the project with deep conviction—as they undoubtedly did—others, notably important segments of the alumni body, were as sincerely committed to fulfilling a plan for which they long had labored.

In April 1968, neither side was quite willing to consider the perspective of the other.

B. *The Institute for Defense Analyses*

Development of the controversy. The Institute for Defense Analyses was established by the Department of Defense and Joint Chiefs of Staff in 1955 in order to obtain organized university research and counsel upon such matters as weapons systems and the conditions of warfare. To a degree, IDA was the Army-Navy counterpart of the Air Force's RAND. At its establishment, five universities became institutional sponsors; seven more joined over the next decade. The Institute employs over 300 research experts at its headquarters in the Washington, D.C. area. Its annual budget is more than $12,000,000.

Columbia became an institutional member of IDA in 1959.

President Kirk and William A. M. Burden, a Trustee of Columbia University, served on both the IDA Board of Trustees and its Executive Committee. The Executive Committee, of which Mr. Burden was Chairman, approved all work conducted by IDA, including classified projects directly related to the prosecution of the Vietnam war. In addition to its full-time employees, IDA engaged individual scholars from different universities to work, under contract, on specific research problems.

Participation by Columbia personnel in IDA projects seems to have been small. Only three faculty members (one an adjunct professor) had ties with IDA. A dozen others, perhaps more, served as consultants at one time or another.

In October 1966, the Independent Committee on Vietnam, a student group whose membership overlapped with SDS, criticized government-sponsored university research on military matters, and demanded the University make public any secret ties to the military or foreign policy establishment. The Administration ignored the call. Student reaction was minimal.

By March 1967, however, there was enough faculty concern about the University's contracts with military and diplomatic agencies to warrant holding a faculty smoker for discussion of the benefits and costs. During the smoker Ralph Halford, then Dean of the Graduate Faculties, was asked some form of question about Columbia's connection with IDA. The University's institutional sponsorship had never been secret. Both its affiliation and the positions held by President Kirk and Mr. Burden were revealed in IDA's annual reports beginning 1960. The reports were all public documents. At the time of the smoker, however, the facts were not widely known, probably because no one had been sufficiently interested for discussion to spread. Dean Halford, who knew the facts and had no reason to withhold them, was understood—or misunderstood—to answer that Columbia had no connection with IDA.

Within a week SDS "disclosed" the "secret" connection uncovered by its research. Thereafter, Dean Halford was reported to have said that at the time of the smoker he had no knowledge of the tie, and to have added:

"I really don't know what IDA does. These things are not

in the purview of faculty and students. . . . This is a matter for the Trustees of the University to decide."

Neither remark attracted widespread contemporaneous interpretation, but both were important, both then and thereafter, in creating distrust for the candor of the Administration and resentment for its alleged indifference toward faculty or student opinion.

SDS immediately passed a resolution calling for disaffiliation from IDA. Both SDS and other critics concerned for the integrity of academic institutions stepped up the campaign against secret research.

Throughout the spring and fall of 1967, Professor of Mathematics Serge Lang sought personal interviews with University officials on such topics as war research, secret contracts, ties with the CIA, and the campus ROTC program. He published his findings in long advertisements in the Columbia *Spectator* in an effort to arouse campus opinion against the war in Vietnam. Because a number of the questions he raised dealt with sensitive and occasionally secret issues, Dr. Lang often did not receive all the information he was seeking to disclose.

One report of an interview with Dean Andrew W. Cordier of the School of International Affairs aroused considerable feeling. Dean Cordier was said to have expressed the belief that none of the School's activities were funded by the CIA. President Kirk had made a similar statement, according to *Spectator,* one week earlier. Since this was about the same time that secret funding arrangements by the CIA had been revealed by *The New York Times* and *Ramparts,* the disclaimers had the effect of partially clearing the Columbia air.*

In October 1967, however, SDS called a news conference to announce that the President and Dean had misstated the facts, that, in truth, for several years, Columbia had received annual grants of $125,000 from the CIA to fund a study of the

---

* We have learned that Dean Cordier told Professor Lang that no classified research was being conducted by the School of International Affairs—which was correct.

economies of East Central European countries, administered by the Office of the Associate Dean. SDS was correct. The contract had been accepted in the mid-1950's during the tenure of Dean Schuyler Wallace, when few scholars and fewer private sponsors were available for this desperately needed research. All research material on the economies of East Central Europe was in the public domain. Several volumes of considerable academic value were produced and rapidly published. The only confidential aspect of the project was the source of its funds—a characteristic of all work then funded by the CIA. At the time of the SDS news conference, Associate Dean Philip E. Mosely and Dean Cordier, who was by then aware of the nature of the original agreement, had already begun negotiations with the CIA to terminate Columbia's connection with the project and publish the facts concerning prior CIA support. Again, although both President Kirk and Dean Cordier may well have sincerely believed that their statements were accurate, their remarks impaired confidence in the Administration both at that time and through constant repetition.

Although the campus as a whole reacted rather casually to the revelations, SDS researchers were able to keep the heat of publicity on the University Administration, which treated the problem of secret war research more casually than its intrinsic difficulty and emotional impact deserved. For example, in the fall of 1967, SDS revealed that in 1964 the Electronics Research Laboratories (ERL), an affiliate of the Electrical Engineering Department, had undertaken IDA-associated secret research in radar detection methods. ERL also had received several million dollars from the Defense Department for undisclosed studies on ballistic missiles.

The relationship of ERL to Columbia was rather complicated but it lent itself to easy if somewhat loose characterization as an arm of the University. In fact, ERL was founded around 1950 by several members of the Electrical Engineering Department, as a separate organization. We are not clear whether they were acting as individuals or for the Department. Later, ERL became an operating facility of the School of Engineering, administered by the Dean's office. Relatively few faculty members participated in the work of ERL and its facilities were not used for instructional purposes, but the Director of ERL was a professor of Electrical Engineering at Columbia and an Associate Dean of the School of Engineering. In November 1967, ERL severed all organizational ties with Columbia and became the Riverside Research Institute. Members of the Columbia faculty still work for RRI and its Board of Directors contains a number of Columbia personnel. We have not sought to determine just where RRI falls in relation to the often fine line between university activities and the private consultation and research of individual professors. In a formal sense, RRI is in the latter category.

In November 1967, SDS revealed that the 432nd Military Intelligence Detachment was engaged in some form of secret research at Columbia, although the nature of its work and ties to Columbia were never made clear. The University thereupon terminated its agreement with the Department of the Army by which office space and library facilities were granted to the 432nd.

Although no single incident appears to have aroused a strong reaction, their cumulative effect was to erode confidence in the Administration's perception and candor in matters relating to secret research. The SDS charges were sometimes distortions; often they were gross oversimplifications. But they had a hard core of substance which was intrinsically important, and the core gave even the penumbra of exaggeration an air of reality. The protest against university complicity symbolized the issues of the Vietnam war, yet provided a more immediate and vulnerable target than the Government. It also attracted the support of academics who, whether hawk or dove, were distressed by any secrecy in university research or any academic dependence upon government contracts serving nonacademic interests.

The issue was by no means confined to Columbia. At Princeton, for example, a committee set up by faculty resolution in November 1967, recommended changing that university's role in the management and activities of IDA. At the University of Rochester there was strong faculty opposition to a $9,000,000 contract with the Center for Naval Analysis. In February 1968, a five-man fact-finding committee recommended that the University of Chicago withdraw its sponsorship of IDA; later Chicago followed the recommendation. Other campuses knew similar controversy.

At Columbia, by early 1968, the IDA question had become SDS' bread-and-butter issue. Because it epitomized all the controversies involved in the Vietnam war, it also became the focus of campus dissent. The earlier questions of class rank and recruiting policy either had been solved or had failed to arouse significant campus support. As the number of relevant issues began to dwindle, the IDA demand received more and more emphasis. The SDS leaders firmly believed that the affiliation was wrong. They were also aware of its potential for politicizing the campus. For both reasons they consciously cultivated the issue. In this one respect, Mark Rudd's October 1967 proposal pointed to the actual program of the organization.*

At the same time the Administration edged toward re-evaluation of its position. In January 1968, President Kirk appointed a faculty committee under the chairmanship of Professor Louis Henkin to study Columbia's external ties and to recommend appropriate action. Early in April the Board of Trustees approved a plan that would terminate Columbia's formal "institutional sponsorship" of IDA, yet have the Board appoint one distinguished member of the University community to serve as a trustee of IDA as an individual. William Burden continued to serve in a wholly private capacity. The announcement of this "disaffiliation" outraged, rather than satisfied, the critics. In terms of the IDA connection, they not unnaturally saw the change as a rather disingenuous attempt to assert severance while continuing the substance of the relationship. In broader terms, they saw the Administration and Trustees as once again attempting an evasive improvisation ignoring student and faculty sentiment.

Appraisal. It would be a mistake to think that in April 1968 the IDA issue had such intrinsic importance as to be listed as a major cause of the magnitude of the disturbances. By itself, it was not a large issue. As a symbol of all the intense antagonism to the Vietnam war, it was many times more im-

---

* See pp. 205–207.

portant. Even then, we think, the issue could have been resolved through the Henkin Committee but for its juxtaposition with other issues in a context of deep-seated dissatisfaction and unrest.*

C. Disciplinary Procedure

On March 27, 1968, SDS organized a demonstration protesting the IDA affiliation that was a deliberate challenge to the "no indoor demonstration" rule. Since the demonstration has already been described,† it is enough to recall that for more than half an hour over 100 students marched about the halls of Low Library chanting slogans and speaking through a bullhorn. Five SDS leaders who were college students and a sixth student in the Graduate School were placed upon disciplinary probation. The SDS rally on April 23, which led, first, to the occupation of Hamilton Hall, and, later to the seizure of other buildings, was called partly to protest this discipline.

The students active in the affair of March 27 unquestionably violated the stated rule against indoor demonstrations, but the Administration's handling of the matter left it vulnerable to four charges that aroused student support for the demonstrators.

1. The rule against indoor demonstrations had been issued by President Kirk himself, in disregard of the unanimous recommendation of his Committee on Student Life (which included Vice-President Truman) without consulting any student organizations.‡

2. The Administration's treatment of indoor demonstrations had been erratic. The ban on indoor demonstrations was not applied to a march of 300 students into Low Library in October 1967. The Dow Chemical demonstration involved an organized march of 100 students into Dodge Hall followed by an 80-man sit-in. No disciplinary action was taken. If neither

---

* We have discussed elsewhere the importance of the way in which some Columbia officials treated the issues. See pp. 44–52.

† See pp. 72–73.

‡ See pp. 50, and 68–69.

of these was an indoor demonstration, what did the rule pro-
hibit? Or, was the Administration unwilling to enforce the
rule, either because the rule was too vague to be administrable
or because it was afraid of a confrontation? The University
community's failure to deal in any way with deliberately offensive personal conduct, such as Mark Rudd's vulgar abuse
of President Kirk, could also be read as weakness. The Administration was undoubtedly seeking to avoid a confrontation
until SDS was so plainly guilty of provocation as to lead the
great bulk of the students to recognize the justice of disciplinary measures, but the improvisation gave an appearance
of weakness that invited youthful challenge. It also pointed
up the inherent ambiguity of the rule and set the stage for
legalistic argument. Later, when the Administration suddenly
reversed its position, the procedural and substantive justice of
its measures was far from obvious.

3. Five college students were disciplined for the IDA
demonstration although about 100 marched in Low Library.
All five were SDS leaders. Were they singled out for political
reprisal against the organization? Dean Platt testified that of
the 100 only those five SDS leaders were recognized. We
accept his word, but to the SDS members and other more
skeptical students the exact coincidence might well have
seemed rather implausible. Furthermore, if the Administration
had wished, it surely could have found a way of identifying
more of the demonstrators during the half-hour they were in
the building.

4. The SDS leaders requested and were refused a public
hearing. The request and refusal focused attention on Columbia's outmoded disciplinary procedure, which provided
for no student participation and vested ultimate disciplinary
power solely in the President. In a period in which public
attention has been focused upon procedural safeguards in
criminal proceedings, students have become rightly concerned
about procedural safeguards in academic discipline. Their
perquisites as students, and, during the current era of selective
military service, their status as students, may even attain life-
or-death importance.

This is not to say that all the requirements for a criminal

trial are appropriate for academic discipline. In most cases, the student offender may fare much better under quasi-parental forms of correction than under a quasi-judicial procedure. But it is one thing to give a choice and another to refuse a public hearing altogether for an offense alleged to have been committed in public, where no one's privacy or reputation can be affected. We are happy to note that, since the April disturbances, there has been much study of Columbia's disciplinary procedures, and they have been considerably strengthened.

Not only was the denial of a public hearing open to criticism, but there was no ready explanation for the failure to deal in some more fundamental way with the entire problem of disciplinary procedures. Resort to improvisation in both the interpretation of the rules affecting demonstrations and the sanctions for their enforcement, instead of attacking a basic weakness, inevitably led to further improvisation with ensuing charges of inconsistency.

During the disturbances the demand for amnesty—for both those who occupied the buildings and those who took part in the March 27 demonstrations—was a central issue. Part of its appeal, although only part, was the feeling that the discipline for the March 27 incident rested upon a shaky foundation.

During the April disturbances there were few, if any, express demands for greater student power. After the buildings were cleared and a strike was called, predominant attention began to focus upon a restructuring of Columbia University that would provide for much greater student as well as faculty participation. We suggested earlier that exclusion from genuine participation in decision-making was one of the basic conditions making for widespread student participation in, and support for, the occupation of the buildings; and for encouragement from many of the junior faculty. The ultimate course of events confirms this view even though the issue lay below the surface in the days immediately preceding the demonstration of April 23.

One final point concerning the three avowed issues should be noted. On none of them had SDS made a genuine effort to exhaust the peaceful forms for shaping a great university's course of action. We are not unmindful that the formal structure of Columbia's institutions, the apparent detachment of the faculty, and the record of the Trustees and Administration made those alternatives such discouraging prospects that no one should be very surprised that they were ignored. Nevertheless, the fact is that on April 23 methods consistent with reason and civility were available and still unused.

III

EVENTS OF APRIL 23–30

A. Demonstration at the Sundial

The front-page headlines of the Columbia *Spectator* for April 22 and 23 flagged the issues. On Monday, April 22, the top left-hand column read:

SDS PLANS MARCH INTO LOW LIBRARY
TOMORROW AT NOON

Below that appeared a three-column head:

VIOLENCE PREDICTED AGAINST CU

The lead said that Harlem leaders had predicted on Saturday that, unless the University stopped construction of the projected gymnasium, "violence may erupt in the Columbia area."

On Tuesday, only the announcement of a new course in Afro-American history broke the universal front page concern with conflict over the gymnasium, IDA, and parietal rules.

CIT COUNCIL AND CORE PLAN
RALLY TO PROTEST NEW GYM

ALUMNUS TO REQUEST
GYM INJUNCTION

GYMNASIUM QUESTION
UNITES LEADING
ACTIVISTS IN HARLEM

BARNARD COMMITTEE
WILL ASK ABOLITION
OF HOUSING RULES

IDA DEMONSTRATORS
PLACED ON PROBATION
ADMINISTRATION MAKES
SECURITY PLANS FOR PROTESTS
ON LOW PLAZA TODAY

MORATORIUM COALITION
ASKS OPEN HEARING
FOR PROTESTERS

The SDS demonstration was scheduled for the Sundial at noon. The *Spectator* advertisement and the only handbill we have seen said that three demands would be presented: (1) that Columbia dissociate itself from IDA; (2) that no discipline be imposed upon those who opposed "Columbia's unjust policies"; and (3) that "those accused" by reason of the March 23 IDA protest receive public hearings before students and faculty "with full rights of due process." Apparently, the gymnasium was not to be an issue on that particular day.

Yet when the demonstration began about noon the presence of black students was noteworthy. SAS and SDS had not previously cooperated. All told, the unusually large crowd numbered about 500 including many curious bystanders as well as the number who intended to challenge the Administration by marching into Low Library. To the north on Low Plaza were stationed about a hundred students opposed to the Sundial demonstrators. Another group of about 50 pickets organized by the Students for a Free Campus stood blocking the path of the proposed march.

The rally began with speeches by Ted Gold and Nick Freudenberg on University discipline and IDA. Cicero Wilson, SAS President, then attacked the construction of the gym-

nasium. Apparently, his participation and the presence of
numerous black students resulted from last-minute consultation. SAS had only recently become concerned with the
gymnasium.°

As Cicero Wilson finished, Dean Platt delivered to the
group a letter from Vice-President Truman offering to meet the
students immediately in McMillin Theatre. There was discussion, and then the crowd agreed by acclamation to accept the
offer only if those who assembled in McMillin were constituted
a "popular tribunal" to judge the students previously disciplined for the March 23 IDA demonstration. Dean Platt declined to reply for the Vice-President.

Mark Rudd then began to speak but the cry was raised, "To
Low, on to Low." The crowd surged up the steps toward Low
Library.† No one can say how many were committed demon-
strators and how many were merely spectators.

As the marchers approached the library, they paused and
swerved to the east, thereby avoiding any serious collision with
the counter-demonstrators gathered at the top of the steps. (It
was later explained that although the marchers far outnumbered their opponents, SDS' quarrel lay with the Administration and not with their fellow students.) A few demonstrators
sought to force entrance through the southeast security door,
but the Administration had had it locked in anticipation of
trouble. Most of the crowd milled around, unsure what to do
next. The demonstration seemed to have lost all sense of purpose. Mark Rudd climbed atop an overturned trash can near
the door and began a rambling discussion of possible courses of
action. Several witnesses recall thinking that SDS had failed
once again in its efforts to mobilize the student body.

° We have been told that flyers were put out before the rally
showing that it would be jointly sponsored by SAS and SDS with
the gymnasium a major issue. Obviously, some agreement for cooperation in the rally was reached, but we have not seen any joint
flyer or other announcement adding the gymnasium to the adver-
tised causes.

† There is testimony that black students were among the leaders
but the photographic evidence seems contradictory. The difference
exemplifies the difficulty of being accurate about all the details of
the disturbances.

But again chance intervened. A voice from the crowd cried for a march to the site of the proposed gymnasium and most of the group, with black students among the leaders, moved eastward toward the excavation at Morningside Drive and 114th Street. A lesser number, among whom were Gold and Rudd, went back to the Sundial for more speeches.

It was 12:30 P.M. when the main body of demonstrators, numbering about 300, arrived at the excavation. Some students began to pull down a section of the fence. Three policemen appeared and tried to block access to the gym site, but they were quickly overwhelmed by the students. More policemen came up; there was a scuffle, and one student was arrested. There was argument over the arrest. A policeman was knocked down and kicked before the students were driven backwards.

At this point Mark Rudd, who had come over to the gymnasium from the campus, stood upon a dirt pile and told Dean Colahan, who also had arrived from campus, that the protesters' demands regarding IDA and the gym would have to be met within 15 minutes. Receiving no answer, he urged the crowd to return to the Sundial. This time the demonstrators responded. On the way back to the campus they encountered the Sundial group which was marching to the gym site. The two groups merged and made their way to the Sundial.

Up to this point, the course of the demonstration had been entirely haphazard. The planned indoor demonstration had not been held. Except for Mr. Rudd's successful effort to avoid further trouble with police at the gym site, the crowd had responded to the calls of unknown members rather than its leaders. The very lack of planning in these early incidents is convincing proof that there was no conspiracy to conduct a sit-in strike or seize a college building. Indeed, the most notable fact is that there was sufficient spirit of unrest—perhaps enough sentiment favorable to SDS—for the demonstrators to hold together despite ineffective leadership. After moments of indecision and frustration at the Sundial, in front of Low Library, and again at the gym site, there was still a crowd of about 500, many of them looking for some kind of showdown with the Administration.

B. *Occupation of Hamilton Hall*

Back at the Sundial, Mark Rudd spoke once. more. He noted that one of the protesters was held as a hostage (apparently referring to the student arrested at the gym site), and suggested that the crowd take a hostage of its own. The meaning of the statement, as reported, seems hardly clear, but the crowd understood it to mean a sit-in and began an orderly march into nearby Hamilton Hall, a classroom building, which also houses the administrative offices of Columbia College. The 450 people who entered the building included opponents of the protest as well as its sponsors and supporters. It was now 1:35 P.M.

The office of the Dean of Columbia College is in Hamilton Hall. Its doors, which open onto the main lobby, had been locked in anticipation of a spill-over from the planned march into Low Library. Dean Coleman himself was out for lunch but he entered the building about ten minutes after the students arrived. The crowd parted, allowing the Dean to reach his door where Proctor William E. Kahn joined him shortly later.

Mark Rudd then presented the demonstrators' demands to Dean Coleman. He added that the Dean would be kept there until some action was taken by the University. Dean Coleman replied that he had no intention of meeting any demands or of calling President Kirk or Dr. Truman under existing circumstances. After some discussion Dean Coleman, Proctor Kahn, and Dan Carlinsky, Director of College Relations, withdrew into the office.

A group of husky students who opposed the demonstration then stationed themselves outside the door. Later, when Dean Coleman emerged briefly, they assured him that they could clear a path for him if he wished to leave, but he declined. This juxtaposition of opposing student factions, with its inherent risk of physical violence, recurred with various degrees of intensity throughout the week that followed. The risk of student combat, with casualties on one side or the other, was a constant source of concern and, ultimately one of the reasons for calling the police to restore order. On this occasion, the risk was one of the factors leading Dean Coleman not to try to leave the building.

At about two o'clock the demonstrators established a ten-man steering committee, half black and half white. The Committee framed six demands:

1) that construction of the gymnasium be stopped
2) that all ties with IDA be discontinued
3) that the ban on indoor demonstrations be rescinded
4) that criminal charges arising out of protests at the gym site be dropped
5) that probation of the "IDA-six" be rescinded
6) that amnesty be granted for the present protest

The students stood upon these demands for the duration of the protest.

Up to this point, except for the somewhat ambiguous restraint upon Dean Coleman, the demonstration did not differ greatly from some earlier incidents. Crowds had milled about in John Jay Hall in protest and support of Marine recruiting. Eighty students had staged the Dow Chemical sit-in in Dodge Hall. This demonstration was larger. Everyone had a vague anticipation of a more serious confrontation, but it is clear that the escalation occurred by small and haphazard steps.

The Commission has heard various accounts of the degree of restraint or lack of restraint imposed upon Dean Coleman. Some participants say that he was always free to leave. Others report that the demonstrators as a body could not agree upon whether to release or detain him, with the result that everyone was left free "to do his own thing." Dean Coleman himself was more than once given the impression that he was not free to go. He testified that about 3:30 P.M. he opened the door of his office and asked whether he was free to leave; when told he was not free, he asked whether the demonstrators would be willing to sign a statement of his detention but they refused. Thereafter the steering committee voted to keep him captive. We have not the slightest doubt that, although there was no formal decision by the whole body of demonstrators, Dean Coleman was deterred from leaving that afternoon, through the night, and part of the next day, by the danger of physical interference with his departure on the part of at least some students.

During the afternoon, Dean Coleman talked by telephone to Dr. Truman and Dean Platt, who were in Low Library. In the absence of President Kirk, who was out of the city, Dr. Truman directed the University's response to the demonstration. His primary concern was to avoid physical conflict between the opposing student factions. Fear of such conflict deterred him from authorizing a group of faculty to enter the building and release the Dean. On the other hand, Dean Coleman himself refused to leave surreptitiously by tunnel, when that seemed a possibility. About 4:30 P.M. Vice-President Truman again sought to defuse the situation with an offer to meet the students, this time in Wollman Auditorium. The demonstrators refused to leave Hamilton Hall.

Outside the Dean's office, in the lobby, a carefree atmosphere prevailed despite the presence of students hostile to the demonstration. A series of speakers occupied the crowd, while other students went out for food and blankets. A rock band later appeared. Entrance and exit remained easy. Regular classes were held in the rooms upstairs. Reports of support from faculty members and from campuses around the city were read and applauded. Ray Brown of SAS and Mark Rudd announced that calls for help had gone out to groups both on and off the campus.

Calling in outside groups with experience in obstructive demonstrations apparently represented a conscious decision on the part of the student leaders to escalate their dispute with the Administration. They rightly surmised that by linking their protest to the sensitive situation in Harlem they would deter intervention by the police because officials would fear that police action might lead to civil disorders. For the white students the price of thus gaining leverage against the Administration was loss of control over the course of the demonstration. The invitations and response were critical turning points in converting a turbulent student protest, that might well have run its course, into six days of forcible student occupation of five college buildings.

Outsiders arrived through the afternoon and evening. About four o'clock Tom Hayden, a founder of SDS who has remained active in radical causes, entered Hamilton Hall, saying that he had heard of the demonstration while at the downtown office. Hayden was in and out of the buildings for the next few days. About six o'clock groups and individuals began to arrive from Harlem and other parts of the city, including representatives from Congress of Racial Equality (CORE), Student Non-Violent Coordinating Committee (SNCC), and other groups. Around eight o'clock, a member of the SNCC declared that "the black community is taking over."

As the evening wore on, the generally light-hearted atmosphere yielded to tension. A group of about eight black youths replaced the anti-demonstrators at the door to Dean Coleman's office. There are reports of a scuffle; whether it occurred or not, the anti-demonstrators got the message. Advised to go, they left the building. About ten o'clock, feelings rose higher when Dr. Truman was reported to have announced that amnesty was "out of the question." This first official comment, prior to any discussion between the Administration and the demonstrators, was taken to indicate the intransigence of the Administration. A little later some students seized a set of janitors' keys to Dean Coleman's office.

Adding to the uneasiness was the report that people from Harlem had brought guns and other weapons into Hamilton Hall. The report, attributed in the newspapers to "reliable witnesses," was widely circulated and universally accepted, but no one we have questioned has told us that he actually saw a gun in Hamilton Hall. Here, as later in the week, rumors and reports assumed a significance independent of objective truth, insofar as they formed the basis for action. The talk of guns was one of the factors that persuaded the University to call on the police for the first time early Wednesday morning.

By late Tuesday evening at least 25 * black people from

---

* This is the only numerical estimate the Commission has been able to obtain. It is unconfirmed and may be too low.

Harlem CORE, SNCC and other groups had arrived. The number was less than some students had hoped to attract, but the black faction was large enough to make its presence felt. Two rooms were appropriated by black students and community people for the storage of food and blankets. They also collected the fire extinguishers within the building, presumably to fight off any efforts to dislodge them.

The process of racial separation within the ranks of the protest accelerated about 2 A.M. on Wednesday, when the steering committee broke into distinct black and white caucuses. Each group met to discuss policies for the coming day. The white caucus on the seventh floor was interrupted by the black group who had decided in favor of blockading the whole building. Some of the whites felt that a blockade would violate the tactical principle established the previous afternoon on Low Plaza because it would place the demonstrators in confrontation with other students rather than the Administration. The consensus of the caucusing whites was that only passage to Administration offices, but not to classrooms, should be obstructed. In the ensuing meeting of the full Steering Committee, the blacks declared that the whites' commitment to the enterprise of confronting the University was inadequate. They asked the white students to leave, and firmly suggested that white students take another building.

Behind the stated ground of the request were deeper reasons. SAS had been apparently seeking an opportunity to demonstrate its discipline and power. Events had precipitated that occasion in advance of planning, but if the occasion was thrust upon them, there it was; SAS would show black power and the issue itself did not matter greatly. In the eyes of the black students, moreover, the SDS crowd seemed sloppy and undisciplined. Their own discipline was almost military and their personal conduct strictly regulated. They feared that the blame for any property damage or untoward incidents would nonetheless be blamed upon the black students.

Regardless of their ability to accept black separatism in a theoretical context, the white students were shocked by their expulsion from the building. Mark Rudd, who announced the black students' decision, was visibly shaken, yet he advocated compliance and others either agreed or felt that no real choice existed.

The white students withdrew from Hamilton Hall about 5:30 A.M. after occupying the building for 16 hours. The 70 black students who stayed began to barricade the entrance. Apparently, some of the outsiders from CORE and SNCC remained with them until later.

C. Occupation of Low Library

After their expulsion from Hamilton Hall the white students gathered outside and decided to seize another building. Two hundred or 250 students went up to Low Library. There they smashed the window of the locked security entrance at the southeast corner of the building, injuring the hand of a security guard. About 150 went on and across the Rotunda where they broke into the President's suite on the west side of the second floor.

Once in the President's office the students, led by SDS, made free with the premises. They played with office equipment, poked into what they pleased, and consumed personal property. There was no substantial vandalism, but the trespasses cannot, even by the wildest stretch be called a form of demonstration. The most serious wrong was the deliberate rifling of President Kirk's files. Some of the papers were photographed and released to the radical press. The participants say that they were searching for evidence of secret links between the University and the military establishment. However just the criticism, these were plainly dishonorable acts.

Not long afterwards a squad of 15 policemen arrived on the scene in response to a call from Captain Adam DeNisco of the Columbia Security Force. By eight o'clock in the morning the number was 35. Word spread inside Low Library that the police were coming and arrest was imminent. Mark Rudd advocated abandonment of the suite and organization of a student strike.* All but 27 fled through the windows. Some

---

* It is worth noting that both at the gym site and on this occasion, Mr. Rudd advocated the more moderate course.

waited outside Low Library. Others gathered in Ferris Booth Hall where an officer of the Citizenship Council made available office space for what was already being called a student "strike" committee. Inside Low Library security guards were permitted to enter the executive suite and remove valuable works of art. The police also went into Dr. Kirk's office, but students remained in the building elsewhere on the second floor.

At this point the demonstration in Low Library could easily have been ended, but nothing was done to evict the remaining students from the rest of the executive suite. Nor were any effective steps taken to bar other students from pouring back into the building and reoccupying the President's office. The attention of both City and University officials was focused upon what was then the far more serious situation in Hamilton Hall.*

Gradually, after the police withdrew from the rooms upstairs, the demonstrators who had fled and probably a good many newcomers went back via the windows into the executive offices. President Kirk's office had been locked but a window was open, accessible by a ledge. The demonstrators added it to the "liberated area." At this time and through most of the week demonstrators passed freely into and out of Low Library and other occupied buildings.

On Wednesday the students inside Low Library engaged in political debate, pursued their "investigation" of the offices, discussed tactics, and amused themselves as best they could. SDS had a meeting in Ferris Booth Hall where tactics were discussed. Mark Rudd, more belligerent than earlier, favored the seizure of additional buildings. Ted Kaptchuk opposed him. During the meeting Mark Rudd announced his resignation as chairman of the Columbia SDS, but the step neither noticeably increased nor diminished his influence.

After the SDS meeting, a Strike Coordinating Committee (SCC) was established. Its steering committee became the governing body of the people in the buildings. Eventually two representatives from each occupied building served on the Steering

---

* See pp. 111–113, and pp. 144–146.

Committee along with an SDS delegation. Hamilton Hall never sent the representatives to which it was entitled and never granted the committee authority to speak for the black students.

During Wednesday there were occasional discussions between the leaders and members of the faculty seeking a solution. They came to nothing and at least one conversation had a harmful effect. Wednesday, probably in the morning, Dean George K. Fraenkel went upstairs in Low Library, joined by Vice-Dean Colahan of Columbia College, and talked with a circle of students at an open door. Mark Rudd was there. Dean Fraenkel argued that, if the leaders were really interested in the substantive demands for changes in the University's policies with respect to the gymnasium and IDA, they should be big enough in spirit to drop the demand for amnesty for individual leaders of the uprising, which the Administration could never grant. In this vein, he said to Mark Rudd, "You, in particular, obviously can expect to be expelled from the University." As the week wore on, this remark and the same assertion by Dean Fraenkel on Thursday, were quoted by students with increasing frequency as evidence that they could not trust any disciplinary procedure short of amnesty because the University was determined to expel the SDS leaders.

D. Occupation of Avery Hall

Wednesday evening students in the School of Architecture took control of Avery Hall, and eventually they barricaded the doors. The sequence of events strongly suggests that much of the uprising and the participation of so many students—the number rose to over 1,000—is to be attributed to a deep-seated and relatively unfocussed dissatisfaction with Columbia life.

Thus, the seizure of Avery Hall did not originate with SDS or even SCC. The Administration, for understandable reasons, ordered all buildings (except dormitories) closed at 6 P.M. on Wednesday instead of leaving them open as usual until 10 or 11 P.M. The architectural students refused to quit work.

The Dean of the School of Architecture and University guards spoke to the students, but no effort was made to dislodge them. Later, the students joined the demonstration. It seems to us that this could not have happened without a much deeper sense of underlying grievance than the trifling irritation of being ordered from the building earlier than usual. Latent dissatisfactions were being quickened by the events in Hamilton Hall and Low Library.

E. *Occupation of Fayerweather Hall*

Early Thursday morning 50 students burst into Fayerweather Hall. The Administration's lack of response flowed from an impression which we discuss later in considerable detail—its belief that the police would not move to protect or reoccupy one building while leaving students in another. This impression, in effect, bound Fayerweather to Hamilton, while Hamilton, by virtue of its occupants, was bound to the black community at large. To clear Fayerweather was to risk chaos in Harlem. No action was taken.

There is every reason to believe that the Fayerweather group, like the architectural students in Avery Hall, were largely independent of SDS. Fayerweather is used chiefly for offices and classrooms for economics, political science, and sociology. The emphasis is on graduate studies, and graduate students made up most of the crowd that came to occupy the building. Some of them had been seeking for a year or more to promote academic changes in these departments.

F. *Response of the Administration*

Early Wednesday morning, long before students had seized Avery or Fayerweather Hall, the Administration realized that even with time and patience the demonstration would not play itself out. About 6 A.M., Dean Coleman, alarmed by the reports of weapons, the eviction of the white students, and the forced entry into Low Library, telephoned Dr. Truman. Dr.

Truman, who had left Low Library only three hours earlier, agreed that mere waiting and offers of discussion might no longer be adequate, and instructed Columbia security officers to call the New York City police. Dr. Truman then returned to the campus where he and President Kirk, who had rushed back to the city, met with two police officials, Assistant Chief Inspector Waithe and Deputy Chief Inspector Taylor. Later they were joined by other City officials, including Commissioner William Booth, Chairman of the Human Rights Commission and Mr. Barry Gottehrer from the Mayor's Office.

Various plans for freeing Dean Coleman were considered and rejected. We appraise them as well as other matters involving actual or projected police intervention in a separate section of this report * because their importance warrants analysis and appraisal in careful detail. Similarly, we reserve for a later section the full analysis of the Administration's and faculty's efforts to find some basis on which the students would leave the buildings without intervention of the police.† Here, we confine ourselves chiefly to the narrative.

All day Wednesday, President Kirk, Dr. Truman, and their advisers concentrated, with the help of City officials, upon finding a peaceful solution to the situation at Hamilton Hall. Both City and University officials, remembering the urban chaos in the summer of 1967 and the riots in other cities following the death of Dr. Martin Luther King, Jr., were deeply worried lest violence at Hamilton Hall grow into a Harlem riot.

On Wednesday morning a young man and a young woman visited Dr. Truman without identifying themselves but they said that they spoke for the students in Hamilton Hall. As he remembers it, no formal demands had then been formulated, but he sent word that the Administration would prefer no criminal charges if the students left the building, gave their names, and submitted to the normal disciplinary procedures.

The Administration formulated a new proposal at a conference on Wednesday afternoon attended by Borough President Sutton, State Senator Patterson, Assemblyman Rangel,

---

* See pp. 158–159.
† See pp. 143–156.

Commissioner Booth, Barry Gottehrer, and President Kirk and Vice-President Truman. The new proposal called for the students to leave the building, give their names, and submit to disciplinary probation for a year. On the question of the gymnasium, President Kirk proposed to call a meeting of the Trustees to consider the resolution adopted by the Faculty of Columbia College earlier that afternoon recommending "immediate suspension of on-site excavation of the gymnasium facility" and "review [of] the matter with a group of community spokesmen" designated by the Mayor.*

The proposal was orally submitted to the black students in Hamilton Hall by Borough President Sutton and his associates, but was not accepted. Later, the substance of the proposal was embodied in a letter signed by Dean Platt and delivered to Hamilton Hall.† When objection was made for want of assurances from President Kirk himself, he sent over a letter which was not only signed by him but which added to the previous proposal.‡ President Kirk then, for the first time, said that he would "recommend favorably" to the Trustees the resolution of the College Faculty; that the disciplinary warning would not bar participation in extracurricular activities, including SAS; and that the University would wipe the students' records clean at the expiration of the period on disciplinary warning. Although Dean Platt had set a 10 P.M. deadline, none was stated by Dr. Kirk.

The black students of Hamilton Hall chose to stay in the building.

G. *Faculty Reaction*

On Wednesday, classes were held as usual in buildings other than Low Library and Hamilton Hall, but individual faculty members became increasingly worried about the disturbance.

---

* The faculty meeting is discussed at pp. 113–114.

† Dean Platt's letter appears as Appendix C, p. 207.

‡ President Kirk's letter appears as Appendix D, p. 208.

Professor Eugene Galanter initiated a petition with the 20 signatures required to call a meeting of the Faculty of Columbia College that afternoon. He then joined a small group which sat discussing the upheaval in the Graduate Students Lounge in Philosophy Hall. There was talk of a need for strong faculty action both to disapprove the students' tactics and to reform the position of the Administration upon the gymnasium, discipline, and other issues of grave student concern. Professors Daniel Bell, Eugene Galanter, and Sidney Morgenbesser, drew up a resolution to be presented to the college faculty that afternoon. The draft "deplored" the seizure of Dean Coleman and "condemned" the invasion of Dr. Kirk's office as well as the rifling of his files. It warned against police action to clear the buildings and advocated a tripartite committee of faculty, students, and administrators to pass upon discipline growing out of the sit-in and upon "other matters of legitimate concern to the University community."

That afternoon the Faculty of Columbia College adopted the draft resolution by an overwhelming vote but not before taking two other significant steps. First, the Faculty rejected, 99–55, a resolution calling for a moratorium on all disciplinary action arising out of the IDA indoor demonstration or the recent disturbances—in short, for amnesty. Second, the Faculty added to the Bell proposal a paragraph in which it petitioned the University immediately to suspend construction of the gymnasium and then to review the whole matter with a group of community spokesmen designated by the Mayor.*

Shortly after the meeting began, Dean Coleman entered the room. His release by the black students in Hamilton Hall and the adoption of the Bell resolution led a number of faculty to believe that the occupation of the buildings would soon be ended. Further cause for optimism was found in the reports, received that afternoon by Dr. Truman, that weapons and outsiders no longer remained in Hamilton Hall. All but a handful of the police who had come onto campus during the morning were withdrawn.

---

* The text of the resolution appears as Appendix E, pp. 209–210.

For some, disappointment followed Wednesday evening when the black students refused to leave Hamilton Hall in response to President Kirk's proposal. Although the Administration never closed its mind to peaceful solutions, after Wednesday night the University officials seem to have felt that the only solution would prove to be calling the police. Some members of the faculty remained more hopeful or, if not hopeful, at least determined to find a solution without the shock of outside police intervention into the academic community. Their efforts were directed along the lines of the Bell resolution.

Since President Kirk had promptly embraced the recommendation concerning the gymnasium, subject to action by the Trustees, nothing could be done on this matter beyond expediting the action of the Trustees. There remained the work of setting up the tripartite committee charged with discussing "disciplinary matters arising out of the incidents yesterday and today, the issue of the gymnasium, and any other matters which are subjects of legitimate concern to the University community." Accordingly, about eleven o'clock Thursday morning an informal group of faculty members meeting in Philosophy Hall requested Professors Eugene Galanter, Carl Hovde, and Lionel Trilling to ask the Administration to take formal steps toward establishing the tripartite committee and defining its jurisdiction and procedures. President Kirk responded by asking the three professors to be an *ad hoc* committee to recommend proposals without binding the Administration to accept their recommendations. The three professors acquiesced and set about their task.

At about 3 P.M. the President and Vice-President held a press conference in Low Library. The thrust of their remarks was that amnesty could not be granted by Columbia without undermining law and order at other institutions, thus indicating no disposition to compromise on a focal point of the dispute. Dr. Kirk also declared that construction of the gymnasium could not be discontinued in the absence of Trustee approval and that the Trustees, whom he had summoned, could not meet on less than three days' notice. The tone sounded harsher on both points than Wednesday's proposal to Hamilton Hall. In a more conciliatory vein, the President announced his appointment of Professors Galanter, Hovde, and Trilling to recommend methods of establishing the Tripartite Commission, but even that concession had to be weighed against his attitude on discipline and evident reluctance to surrender his ultimate authority over all discipline.

Professor Alan F. Westin had, by this time, assumed a measure of leadership in the faculty group meeting informally in Philosophy Hall. He had protested the failure to invite members of the faculty to the press conference and obtained space for a few. Now he induced Dr. Truman to visit Philosophy Hall to explain the University's position to about 125 faculty members who had gathered there, making a special effort to circulate word to all faculty members through secretaries in the various departments. Dr. Truman was questioned about the University's stake in continuation of construction of the gymnasium. When he estimated that breach of the building contracts would cost Columbia $6,000,000 in damages, several of those present took strong exception. After he left, Professor Westin, who was disturbed by the hardening position of the Administration, remarked that the faculty's admiration for the Vice-President was blinding it to the need for action on its own part. Professor Walter Metzger then suggested that the meeting continue with Professor Westin in the chair.

The ensuing discussion led to the formation of the Ad Hoc Faculty Group (AHFG). The premise shared by its founders was the belief that a strong segment of the faculty, acting informally and independently, could effect a settlement of the dispute. Its charter was this resolution, drawn up at the meeting:

We, the undersigned members of the Columbia University Faculty and teaching staff make the following proposal to resolve the present crisis:

1) We request the Trustees to implement the immediate cessation of excavation on the gymnasium site, by telephone vote if necessary.

2) We request the Administration to delegate all disciplinary power on matters related to the present crisis to the tripartite committee, consisting of students, faculty, and Administration.

3) We request the students to exacuate all buildings now, and we pledge our faith and influence towards a solution. Should the students be willing to evacuate the buildings, we will not meet classes until the crisis is resolved along the above lines.

4) Until this crisis is settled, we will stand before the occupied buildings to prevent forcible entry by police or others.

By seven-thirty Thursday evening, 150 senior and junior faculty and some teaching assistants had signed the resolution. AHFG decided that junior faculty members would be allowed to attend and vote at its meetings, although they did not enjoy these privileges at formal proceedings of the various Columbia Faculties. During the following days, when the group was convened in more or less continuous session, there was sometimes only erratic checking of credentials to speak or vote. Whoever was present had a full voice in the debate.

Emissaries from AHFG immediately fanned out to inform the various parties of the role AHFG projected. Hamilton Hall, in a press release issued about nine o'clock Thursday evening, restated the black students' demands:

1) end construction of the gymnasium
2) amnesty
3) sever ties with IDA
4) drop prosecution of demonstrators arrested at the gym site

but their statement also noted with approval "the positive efforts of the Ad Hoc Faculty Group."

The Strike Steering Committee (SCC) sent a delegation to plead its case before AHFG in Philosophy Hall, where the students argued that their demands with respect to IDA and the gymnasium should be granted immediately, and that they should not be punished for pressing "legitimate demands against the illegitimate authority of the Administration." There were questions but no negotiation. During the meeting Dean Fraenkel repeated his earlier observation that Mark Rudd could surely expect to be expelled. These remarks were later cited to show that SCC could never rely upon any compromise on the issue of amnesty or discipline.°

Thursday evening, while some of its members were trying to lay a basis for negotiations, AHFG continued to meet informally in Philosophy Hall. There was great tension on the campus and a series of threatened outbreaks of violence had required AHFG attention.† About 1:30 A.M. on Friday, Dr. Truman appeared in the room. Tired by strain, lack of sleep, and conflicting emotions, his manner was curt. He announced, first, that bands of students had just seized Mathematics and Lewisohn Halls ‡ and, second, that the police would shortly clear the buildings. The faculty present were shocked. If there were no cries of "Shame" as reported in the press, there surely was hot opposition. Dr. Truman left almost at once. Professor Westin, joined by Professor Alexander Dallin and others, followed him to Low Library in an effort to induce a change of plan. The emotional tension of the scene is beyond our powers of description.

H. *Police Intervention: Plan and Cancellation*

The Administration's decision should not have been surprising. Hamilton Hall had been barricaded for a day and a half. Low Library had also been occupied for that period.

° We discuss at pp. 148–155, whether the response from the buildings gave solid ground for AHFG negotiations.

† See pp. 121, 135.

‡ Actually, a rather different situation had developed at Lewisohn Hall. The building, used primarily by students and faculty of the School of General Studies, had been "liberated" to prevent the seizure by other demonstrating students so that the Lewisohn Hall students could proceed with their normal academic work.

First Avery, then Fayerweather, and then Mathematics Hall
had been seized by students. The number of students and supporters in each building, except Hamilton Hall, was constantly
rising, so that the danger increased even when the number of
occupied buildings remained the same. None of the demonstrating students gave substantial evidence of willingness to
leave unless the Administration and Trustees acquiesced in
their demands.

The turmoil on the campus became an even greater danger.
The seizure stirred reaction toward even more serious violence.

On Wednesday a group calling itself the "Majority Coalition" had gathered signatures—2,000 signatures it announced—
to a petition that stated:

> We, the undersigned, students at Columbia University
> deplore the tasteless, inconsiderate, and illegal manner in
> which the protests of April 23 and 24 against the Institute
> for Defense Analyses and construction of the new gym
> were conducted. We believe such outrageous conduct to be
> completely contrary to the best interests of Columbia Uni-
> versity and her students. We urge the Administration to take
> firm action to prevent a recurrence of the deplorable dis-
> ruption and to punish severely those responsible for it.

All day Thursday students aligned with the Majority Coalition became increasingly impatient with the Administration's
inaction in the face of spreading disruption. Several hundred
students, among whom athletes were prominent, met in the
old gymnasium during the early afternoon, and a number expressed their readiness to "clean out" the occupied buildings.
Jack Rohan, the coach of Columbia's highly successful basket-
ball team, calmed the audience somewhat by a forceful speech,
pointing out that what distinguished his audience from the
people in the buildings was respect for rules and disdain of
physical force. Dean Coleman, who had consulted President
Kirk just before the meeting, spoke next. A former crew coach,
he furnished liaison between the Administration and the conservative portion of the student body during the year. He told
the audience that, if negotiations with Hamilton Hall had not

settled the dispute by six o'clock, "definitive action" would be taken by the President. Dr. Kirk had told the Dean that the "action" he would request would be police intervention, but the Dean did not elaborate his meaning. Dean Coleman's announcement helped to satisfy those who wanted action, but it also created expectations whose subsequent disappointment would revive the demand for self-help.

About 9 P.M. there was another intense moment. Several Harlem groups had called for a rally at 116th Street and Broadway, one of the two main entrances to the campus. Upwards of 1,000 spectators and 200 policemen were present. It was a mixed group, some favoring and some hostile to the University. Among them were Columbia students opposed to the strike who were again growing restive as a result of what they saw as the Administration's inaction. When speakers criticized Columbia's proposed gymnasium and attitude towards her neighbors, this group responded with heckling and epithets. Tension grew to a climax when at the end of the rally Charles 37x Kenyatta, the leader of Harlem's "Mau Mau" group, called for a march eastward across College Walk in defiance of the hostile students.

Dean Coleman, addressing the students with a bullhorn advised them to stand their ground: "This is your property." Physical contact seemed unavoidable, for Kenyatta could not yield. Chief Waithe, turning to Dean Coleman, advised him to let the march proceed, and the Dean had the wisdom to counsel the students again to exercise restraint. Violence was avoided when the students gave way in the face of the Dean's persuasion and the calm pressure of city policemen, who cleared a path for the march. The marchers traversed the campus and peacefully disbanded.°

° The incident is a good example of wise and knowledgeable police action. Mr. Kenyatta was anxious to avoid violence but he had called his followers to action, thus making it politically impossible for him to withdraw without doing something dramatic. A march across the campus filled the bill, and he thought he could accomplish it and lead his followers from the scene without the outbreak he sought to avoid. Apparently, Chief Waithe realized Mr. Kenyatta's predicament.

Anger and resentment continued to grow among students opposed to the strike. About 10 P.M. a large group, including varsity athletes and signers of the Majority Coalition's petition, assembled in front of Fayerweather Hall. "Definitive action" was promised, but nothing had been done. Now they would eject the strikers from the building with their own hands. A violent student assault upon the demonstrators who had barricaded themselves in Fayerweather Hall was imminent when members of AHFG hurried to the scene from their meeting in Philosophy Hall. By a combination of physical interposition and attentiveness to the moderates' complaints, they warded off the invasion after some jostling between the student factions. A professor singled out one, student to choose four others as delegates to AHFG. The five then returned to Philosophy to explain their position to the AHFG membership at large. The delegates sent their followers to Wollman Auditorium to await the outcome of the meeting.

In Wollman the crowd, consisting mostly of the Majority Coalition and its allies, debated the most effective way to express opposition to the strike. There was still sentiment for self-help. When the delegation to the AHFG returned, however, it was accompanied by Professors C. Lowell Harriss, Orest Ranum, and Warner Schilling, whose speeches calmed the crowd. Professor Schilling praised the restraint shown thus far by the students present and contrasted their appreciation of the importance of reason and civility with the demonstrators' evident contempt for restraints necessary to liberty. Yet the audience was not fully satisfied until it received word that the police had been summoned, shortly after Dr. Truman made the same announcement in Philosophy Hall.

Dr. Truman's announcement, as we have seen, met strong opposition. On Wednesday, the Faculty of Columbia College had expressed its belief that:

> any differences have to be settled peacefully, and we trust that police action will not be used to clear Hamilton Hall or any other University building.

Perhaps the swift development of the crisis had outmoded that part of Wednesday's resolution, but verbally it stood as the expression of the Faculty's will. Furthermore, on Thursday evening, AHFG had constituted itself upon the promise:

> Until this crisis is settled, we will stand before the occupied buildings to prevent forcible entry by police or others.

Upon hearing the announcement that the police had been called, AHFG members moved out from Philosophy Hall to posts before the occupied buildings where they would block the police called by the University Administration to evict demonstrators who had unlawfully seized and barricaded the University buildings.

About half-past two in the morning a dramatic and much debated incident occurred. A group of men, perhaps 20 or 30, pushed through the crowd toward the southeast entry of Low Library, which gave access to the temporary offices being used by the Administration. The AHFG cordon blocked their path and called upon them for identification. The men were not ordinary plainclothesmen, as many have supposed, but middle-echelon police officers who had been called by their superiors to help prepare detailed plans for clearing the buildings. Many AHFG members were young instructors; it is unlikely that the police officers knew who they were or by what authority they were blocking the path to the office to which the police had been summoned. The police officers pushed ahead. A scuffle followed. Some say that nightsticks flailed, drawn from under the coats of the policemen. Richard Greeman, an instructor, was cut on the head. He is convinced that it was done with a weapon. The police deny the use of weapons and suggest that Greeman fell, as the police shoved through, and cut his head on the walk. The police officers were of such rank and upon such a mission that they would not have been carrying nightsticks under their coats, but some might have had other weapons. The transcendent fact is that violence is virtually certain to occur when, in an emotional environment, one group moved by its conscience undertakes physically to obstruct another group which is, in equally good conscience, performing its civic duty.

Greeman withdrew into Low Library bleeding profusely from a scalp wound it took four stitches to close. There, Professors Dallin and Westin, together with Dean Fraenkel, pleaded for reconsideration of the decision to call the police, stressing AHFG's need for time to effect a settlement. The injury to Mr. Greeman dramatized the dangers of police intervention in the face of faculty opposition so intense as to find expression in a physical cordon blocking access to the buildings. The Administration yielded.

Inside the building, Administration officials continued to confer with members of the faculty on the consequences of the change in plan. At about 3:15 A.M. Dr. Truman walked out of the southeast security door and addressed a large crowd of students and teachers:

> The Faculty Committee has persuaded the University Administration to postpone a request for police action on the campus while the faculty and the Administration continue their efforts to effect a peaceful solution to the situation. Necessary security arrangements will of course be maintained. To encourage these efforts, the University will be closed until Monday.
>
> At the request of the Mayor, and without prejudice to continuation at a later time, we have suspended construction on the gymnasium pending further discussions.

The suspension of construction had been arranged that afternoon after a telephone poll or informal gathering of the Trustees without the formal three-days notice.

The postponement of police intervention gave time for AHFG to attempt, by mediation or otherwise, to work out a peaceful solution. We follow those efforts next, before returning to the events on the campus.

I. *Efforts At Peaceful Resolution*

AHFG efforts to establish a basis for voluntary evacuation of the buildings followed the lines of the Wednesday resolution of the College Faculty and Thursday's AHFG statement. But since the University officials had gone very far to comply

with the recommendations on the gymnasium, disciplinary
proceedings became the focus of attention.

On Friday, Professors Galanter, Hovde, and Trilling
brought in a tentative report on their work as an *ad hoc* committee to make recommendations on the implementation of
the College Faculty's call for a tripartite committee:

> A tripartite body to discuss any disciplinary matters arising
> out of the incidents yesterday and today, the issue of the
> gymnasium and any other matters which are subjects of
> legitimate concern to the University community.

They had chosen to concentrate upon discipline. They
recommended a committee composed of five faculty, five
students, and two administrators which would formulate general disciplinary measures for various classes of conduct
arising out of the seizure of the buildings, rather than determine penalties in individual cases. Actual penalties would be
dispensed by the Administration, as previously, but appeal
would lie to the Tripartite Committee. The status of its decisions was left uncertain, although the *ad hoc* committee apparently intended no further review. In its final form submitted
Sunday, the Committee's letter to the President stated:

> We envisage that the decisions of the Commission acting
> on its appellate capacity will be binding on all parties but
> we recognize the statutory responsibilities of the President.*

On Friday, the Administration made no comment upon the
Galanter-Hovde-Trilling proposal. The demonstrators found
it less than an assurance of amnesty, and to that extent unacceptable. During the small hours of Friday morning, Professors
Westin, Silver, and Rothman had a long, private meeting with
Messrs. Gilbert, Rudd, and Gonzales of SCC. They met again
in Ferris Booth Hall on Friday afternoon. The SCC repre-

---

* The letter also urged President Kirk to "remind" the University community that work on the gym had been suspended and
that the IDA issue was in the hands of Professor Henkin's Committee.

The Galanter-Hovde-Trilling proposal formed the basis of the
AHFG's negotiating efforts during the afternoon and evening.

sentatives made neither proposals nor concessions. They constantly reasserted the same six demands without the least modification. Sometimes they added other demands such as that President Kirk should resign. If there was the slightest reason for supposing that they were willing to find a basis for compromise, it lay in their demeanor and the questions they asked about AHFG suggestions. There was no "give" in their negotiating position. The AHFG spokesmen focused much of their attention upon persuading the SCC representatives that, since the demand for amnesty would never be supported by the faculty, it should be dropped in favor of guarantees adequate to bar heavy reprisals and protect the leaders from discrimination.

By Friday night, with amnesty isolated as the critical issue, the prospects for settlement came to turn upon politics within the strike movement, and in particular upon Fayerweather Hall. As the building with the largest and most moderate population, it was likely that "Fay" would be readier than the others to compromise on the theretofore inviolate six demands. In a vote taken on Friday, Fayerweather dropped the requirement of outright amnesty in favor of "equal treatment of all student participants, regardless of [their] role in [the] strike," with "all disciplinary action to terminate by the end of the academic year." Its advocates viewed this proposal as a gesture to AHFG which would line up the faculty behind the strikers' remaining demands while leaving the students vulnerable only to minimal punishment. They also argued that it would allow the Administration to save face on the matter of discipline.

Fayerweather's representatives reported the vote to SCC on Friday night. The opponents of their plan gave a different forecast of faculty response. A majority of SCC felt that the AHFG could be brought to support amnesty and that the Administration would then have to buckle. Students at Howard University, it was pointed out, had established a precedent by winning amnesty in an analogous situation earlier in the spring. An inconsistent but parallel reason for firmness was also advanced: the faculty lacked power, so compromise to win its sympathy would be wasted. Others thought that com-

promise would be mistaken for weakness rather than reason-
ableness. Those concerned with pure ideology argued that
to submit to any punishment would be to acknowledge the
authority of an Administration that was illegitimate.

Professors Westin, Silver, and Rothman met again with
Messrs. Gilbert, Rudd, and Gonzales from 11 P.M. Friday
night on into Saturday morning. The students vigorously challenged the statement that the faculty was strongly opposed
to amnesty. A large part of AHFG's shifting membership was
favorable to the SCC position. SCC was well aware of this
opinion and either hoped to split the faculty or mistook the
breadth of opposition to this form of demonstration. The conversation was broken up when Professor Peter B. Kenen
summoned the AHFG negotiators back to Philosophy Hall because he sensed that AHFG was about to vote on the question
of amnesty. The AHFG negotiators, accompanied by Mark
Rudd, rushed back to the meeting. Professor Westin reported
that the conversations with SCC made him cautiously opti-
mistic. Mark Rudd asked to speak. He asserted that talks
were useless unless AHFG would support amnesty and described Professor Westin's report as "bull-shit." AHFG was
visibly shocked by Mr. Rudd's manners. The body voted confidence in its negotiators and adjourned.

Later that morning Messrs. Gonzales, Gold, and Freudenberg of SCC met with Professors Silver and Fogelson. They
apologized for Mr. Rudd's conduct and resumed discussion
of the issues. Not the slightest progress was made, however,
and it is doubtful that progress was intended. The prevailing
SCC view was that the faculty should be politicized and then
give its support to SCC demands.

Two other events on Saturday dimmed hope for a peaceful
solution. First, a morning caucus in Fayerweather overturned
the previous day's proposal to drop the demand for amnesty.
Second, William E. Peterson, Chairman of the Board of
Trustees, released a statement which virtually eliminated
whatever slight chance there was of arranging a voluntary
withdrawal. The statement gave the Trustees' wholehearted
support to the refusal of amnesty and called upon President
Kirk not to relinquish ultimate disciplinary power. The Trust-

ees also stated that the gymnasium was not a racial issue, thus setting themselves in opposition to a large body of student and faculty opinion and raising doubts about the seriousness of the promised review.

The President's ultimate disciplinary power was an especially sensitive point. The demonstrating students felt that they needed protection against the discrimatory or vindictive use of disciplinary power. Some, including Mark Rudd, had engaged in calculated obscenities that would have tried the most charitable spirit. Many were persuaded that the five SDS leaders were singled out for punishment after the IDA demonstration on March 28 because they were SDS leaders and not because Dean Platt could recognize no others. Dean Fraenkel had twice publicly stated that, whatever else happened, Mark Rudd would be expelled. Other SDS leaders must have supposed that they could hardly expect less severe penalties. After the IDA incident of February 1967, President Kirk had used his final authority to increase the punishment recommended by a tripartite group (although he decreased it in another). The University statutes could be said to require the President to exercise final authority; but that was hardly a necessary legal conclusion. The thought behind the Hovde-Galanter-Trilling report was that he would commit himself not to exercise whatever power was formally acknowledged. The conversations with SCC leaders made it obvious to anyone familiar with their direction that this concession was indispensable to any voluntary withdrawal from the buildings.

Dr. Frode Jensen, a member of the Board of Trustees, was reported in Sunday's *Spectator* to have declared that the aim of the statement was to undercut any student-faculty negotiations inconsistent with the University statutes vesting disciplinary power in the President. If that was the aim, it was indeed accomplished. All the subsequent discussions over ways of settling the problem of discipline fell under the shadow of the Trustees' declared position.

SCC's Saturday night meeting produced signs of friction within the strike movement but no real change. During the afternoon the students in Fayerweather Hall again reversed their position and favored modification of the amnesty demand.* Fayerweather had also dispatched emissaries to the other buildings to urge acceptance of the modification. Low refused even to admit the emissaries according to one witness.

Discussion at the SCC centered on whether talks with AHFG should be resumed. Although the representatives from Avery, Mathematics, and Fayerweather favored resumption, Low was opposed. Since it had been agreed that any change in SCC's position would require unanimity, Low's representatives had their way.

About midday Sunday, SCC issued a statement explaining that the faculty's lack of power, as evidenced by the Trustees' statement concerning discipline, made further negotiations useless and it called upon the faculty to take a political stand on the amnesty issue.

That evening SCC held another meeting on strategy. In an afternoon vote, Fayerweather, while still unwilling to violate the solidarity of the movement by negotiating separately, had nonetheless overwhelmingly voted to revive its earlier plan to modify the amnesty demand. "Revolutionaries," argued Fayerweather, "don't demand amnesty from an illegitimate authority." "The general answer to Fayerweather," the minutes of the meeting say, "was that amnesty was not being demanded from the present powers; that we are not in a revolutionary situation; that the fight for amnesty makes the formal structure real by politicizing the students and making our position crystal clear; that the new structures may have to be acted against and that a political principle must be established of being able to act against illegitimate authority; that we are becoming stronger and stronger and that time had not yet come for negotiations, if there ever was a time; and that we are seeking to form a radical faculty group which will encourage the faculty to move toward the left."

AHFG, struck from one side by SCC adamancy and from the other by the Trustees' announcement, turned away from private negotiations to what one of its members described as

---

* It was explained to us that voting attendance at meetings varied with the hour. The smaller groups that came early in the morning contained a larger proportion of radicals than those that met in the afternoon.

"public mediation," thus denoting an effort to formulate a just solution, build public support, and thereby compel the parties to accept it. The AHFG steering committee labored through the early hours of Sunday morning in order to prepare a statement that might be accepted by AHFG before a joint meeting of all the Columbia Faculties in Morningside Heights, which had been called for 10 A.M. that morning.° The statement had four major parts. One dealt with discipline. It recommended:

—establishment of the Tripartite Commission
—immediate revision of the University statutes to vest final power over discipline in the Tripartite Commission
—acceptance of a principle of collective responsibility for infractions during the crisis so that all violators of the discipline of the University would receive identical treatment.†

The second part dealt with the gymnasium. The resolution noted the suspension of construction and proposed the formation of a panel to review the project, consisting of representatives of the Trustees, the faculty, and the community, with the latter group chosen by Mayor Lindsay and given a veto over any construction of a gymnasium in Morningside Park. The proposed community veto was a new element.

Third, the resolution called upon the students, if President Kirk accepted the first two proposals, to vacate the buildings and submit themselves to discipline under the proposed procedure.

Finally, the resolution declared:

These proposals being in our judgment a just solution to

° The full text appears as Appendix F, pp. 212–213.

† Although there was some discussion of the abstract merit of this principle, it was essentially a euphemistic formula for promising the student leaders that they would be neither suspended nor expelled. The underlying assumption was that neither of those penalties could be applied to several hundred students.

the crisis our University is presently undergoing, we pledge that

a. If the President will not adopt these proposals, we shall take all measures within our several consciences to prevent the use of force to vacate these buildings.
b. If the President does accept our proposals but the students in the buildings refuse to evacuate these buildings, we shall refuse further to interpose ourselves between the Administration and the students.

The exact meaning of these last two points is pivotal, but unclear. Under one reading, the resolution omitted any statement with respect to AHFG action in the event that neither the Administration nor the students accepted its recommendations. Under another reading, AHFG pledged members, to the limit of their individual consciences, to prevent intervention by the police unless President Kirk accepted the recommendations, regardless of the action of the rebellious students. At least some of the students and a number of AHFG members accepted the second interpretation. One prominent member gave this explanation to strike leaders.

A little later Sunday morning there was an unprecedented joint meeting of all the Faculties on Morningside Heights. The call for the meeting had itself sparked debate over whether junior members excluded from the several Faculties under long-standing Columbian practice should be allowed to attend. AHFG had admitted junior members and they carried weight in its deliberations. As a group the junior members were more politically-minded and much more sympathetic to the uprising than the typical senior professor. The Administration opposed the participation on the ground that no meeting place of adequate size was available. Many faculty members doubted the sincerity of the explanation. The debate consumed a disproportionate amount of time. Whether a compromise agreement was reached, is itself a matter of disagreement. The real significance of this conflict lies, first, in the antagonism that the Administration's position engendered just when the University needed all possible support, and, second, in the further evidence it supplies of the extent to which the ancient exclusion of the junior

faculty from participation in decisions had alienated a vital
segment of the University community.

At the meeting the Morningside Faculties adopted, 466–40,
a resolution prepared by Professors Kenen and Sigmund
Diamond.° The motion "condemned the violence that has occurred, including the occupation of buildings and disruption
of normal University activities." It commended the suspension
of excavation at the gym site, endorsed the Tripartite Commission, and recognized the vital services of AHFG members. It
also expressed "deep appreciation of the patience and restraint shown by the Administration" and called upon the students occupying University buildings to recognize that failure
to resolve the crisis rapidly and peaceably "may result in irreparable damage to all members of this community." There
was nothing explicit about use of the police, yet the tone
seems markedly different from the College Faculty's Wednesday resolution and the AHFG resolution adopted only a few
hours before.†

On Sunday, AHFG widely publicized its proposal and
sought to obtain endorsements from every possible source.
Ultimately it was signed by 797 faculty members, students,
and a number of widely-known public figures.

President Kirk announced the University's response on
Monday, April 29. He noted that work on the gymnasium had
been halted by the Trustees and promised to go forward with
discussions with City officials and community leaders. His
statement obviously avoided any commitment either to abandon the project or to give community representatives a veto
over recommencement of the work.

On discipline, President Kirk accepted the Tripartite Commission and referred the matter of uniform penalties to the

---

° The full text is set out as Appendix G, pp. 214–215.

† One would expect the Joint Faculties to be somewhat more
conservative than the College Faculty alone because the former
comprised teachers of the professions as well as those of the liberal arts. Yet this will not explain the 466–40 vote. Probably the
explanation is that no one could really find anything objectionable
in the Kenen-Diamond resolution, and no one wished a bitter controversy over matters left unsaid.

Commission as had been recommended in the Galanter-Hovde-Trilling report.* With respect to the finality of the decisions of the Tripartite Commission, President Kirk announced:

> I will recommend to the Trustees that the statutes of the University dealing with disciplinary matters be re-examined in the light of the recommendations submitted by the tripartite commission.

The statement left President Kirk's own position ambiguous with respect to the finality of tripartite review. The Trustees' attitude, on the face of their Saturday statement, seemed obvious, although one could argue that the real purpose of the statement was not to judge a specific issue but to support the President in a crisis. While the indulgent observer might conclude that the University officials had moved a long way toward accepting the AHFG solution, the harsh and distrusting critic could equally well conclude that in the final analysis the assurances came to very little.

SCC did not move at all. We have been told that SCC never seriously considered accepting the AHFG solution, but that it was discussed in terms of propaganda so that the response might attract the strongest sentiment to the side of the rebel students if and when the police were summoned. Accordingly, SCC issued two statements, one Sunday, rejecting the AHFG solution, and the second Monday, commenting on the statement issued by President Kirk. The second argued:

> We striking students reaffirm our six demands, including amnesty. Amnesty must be a precondition for negotiations. Our demand for amnesty implies a specific political point. Our actions are legitimate; it is the laws and the Administration's policies, which the laws have been designed to protect, that are illegitimate. Almost everyone has agreed

---

* Sunday afternoon, Professors Galanter, Hovde, and Trilling had formally submitted the recommendations on the composition, jurisdiction, and procedures of the tripartite committee on disciplinary matters announced Friday morning. They included the names of students, professors and administrators who they thought should serve on the committee.

that the underlying cause of the present crisis has been the policies and procedures imposed by the Administration. Faculty apathy also has allowed this condition to exist.

AHFG could do no more to avert catastrophe. It somewhat frantically debated proposals to ask Governor Rockefeller or Mayor Lindsay to mediate. Unfortunately, but quite humanly, the group never faced up to the question what should the faculty do, or bring the Administration to do, in order to minimize the risk of physical violence and resulting outrage in the case of police intervention.

We should note one other effort at mediation centered upon Hamilton Hall. Dr. Kenneth Clark, an eminent social psychologist who knew a number of the black students, went to Columbia on Saturday out of concern for their welfare and, if possible, to ease the situation. On Monday afternoon Theodore Kheel, an experienced mediator, entered Hamilton Hall with Dr. Clark and, after receiving assurances that the black students were genuinely interested in searching for a negotiated withdrawal, he evolved the following proposal:

1. The students should recognize that the vote which the Trustees had by then adopted to suspend the construction of the gymnasium, represented substantial accomplishment of the students' major objective.
2. The students should leave the building after identifying themselves and submit to normal university discipline.
3. The disciplinary measures imposed by the University should be subject to review by an outside Board of Arbitration.
4. The students should be free to return to classes and participate fully in all normal university activities pending disciplinary proceedings and all appeals.

It was then afternoon. The black students took the plan under advisement, promising a response by 8 P.M. (Later, the time was extended to 11 P.M.) With this hope of progress, Dr. Clark and Mr. Kheel took their proposal to the Administration. The suggestion of review by a Board of Arbitrators was thought by Dr. Kirk to fly in the face of his responsibility

to enforce discipline under the University statutes—an authority that the Trustees two days earlier had called upon him to
assert in the strongest terms.° There was talk of his retaining
such power "as the law required," while recognizing that in
practical effect he would be bound by the Board's decisions.
President Kirk would not accept the plan, but neither did both
he and Dr. Truman quite reject the idea of the Clark-Kheel
solution if the black students would agree. The matter was
left open for further discussion once the black students'
answer was received.

    Dr. Clark and Mr. Kheel had planned next to submit their
suggestion to the Strike Coordinating Committee, but they
refrained pending the receipt of word from Hamilton Hall.

    About 10:45 P.M. the black students notified Dr. Clark that
they rejected the proposal. One can only speculate about the
reasons. By this time Inspector Waithe had had a number of
conversations with black students inside Hamilton Hall. The
black students had decided and the police knew that, if the
police were asked to clear Hamilton Hall, the black students
would submit to arrest and leave with dignity. Throughout
the week they acted with restraint. Under these circumstances
they might well have thought that there was little to be gained
by voluntary settlement. In addition, although the black students were anxious to emphasize their racial independence,†
some may have been a little reluctant to desert the demonstrators in the other buildings.

    Although Hamilton Hall did not ordinarily send representa-
tives to meetings of the SCC Steering committee, a spokesman
appears to have been present at Monday's SCC meeting and
he assured the group that despite talk of an "autonomous"

    ° See p. 127.

    † Thus, a Hamilton Hall press release issued Sunday evening
asserted:

    Contrary to what has recently been reported the Hamilton
    Hall occupation is an autonomous Black Student demon-
    stration against Columbia University's high-handed en-
    croachment on Harlem. We and our community supporters
    are determined to put a halt to Columbia's racist policies.

demonstration in its Sunday press statement, Hamilton would not accept amnesty for itself unless the other buildings were included.

Whatever the reasons it was plain on Monday night that negotiation and mediation were dead.

J. Conditions on Campus, April 26–30

While AHFG negotiators struggled to find a peaceful solution, other members of the group dealt with the problems of maintaining a semblance of order on the campus lest violence break out among students.

The Majority Coalition was still restive. Its supporters lost faith in Dean Coleman when the promised "definitive action" failed to materialize. Friday, Professor Warner Schilling urged AHFG to approve a faculty blockade preventing free entry into Low and require those leaving to surrender their Columbia identification cards and submit themselves to discipline. He believed that the restriction would mollify the Coalition and reduce the danger of conflict. AHFG reestablished its cordon but later confusion arose as to whether identification cards had to be surrendered and the requirement was dropped. AHFG patrols stationed at either end on College Walk required identification of people seeking to enter the campus.

Tense incidents continued to occur. Late Friday morning a contingent of black high school students swept onto campus through the police lines. Some tried to enter Hamilton, but were barred by the students inside who told them to "cool it." The teenagers massed on South Field but gradually dispersed.

Within an hour, H. Rap Brown and Stokely Carmichael arrived with a group of followers who were probably more high school students. Brown and Carmichael were admitted to Hamilton Hall where they remained for forty minutes. Upon emerging, Brown emphasized to a crowd gathered outside the importance of the black students' demands and action, but his demeanor made it plain that the students were conducting their own action.

The Coalition held a meeting late that Friday afternoon in

Wollman Auditorium. Its chairman, Paul Vilardi, had previously spoken out in favor of the proposed Tripartite Committee. At the meeting, Professor C. Lowell Harriss suggested that its members demonstrate their support of the faculty's mediation efforts by a silent march to Philosophy Hall. The Majority Coalition's stance at this point was broad enough to encompass all shades of opinion not in agreement with the SCC methods; it contented itself with condemning disruption as a method of resolving issues such as the construction of the new gymnasium and Columbia's affiliation with IDA. For all that, the Coalition kept a reputation as a conservative faction, rather than a moderate group.

While the Coalition was meeting in Wollman, a large number of New York City police gathered at Amsterdam Avenue and 116th Street. At about 6:00 P.M. Friday, they were deployed to various points throughout the campus. The police emphasized that their purpose was to maintain peace on campus, but not to clear the buildings. Their arrival did nothing to lessen the emotional tension.

On Friday night still another rally was conducted at 116th Street and Broadway. Speakers again condemned the gymnasium project and Columbia's neighborhood policies. This time, however, there was no confrontation between students and community groups.

We do not stop to relate all the statements and counterstatements issued by political groups, but our attention to conflict between the Majority Coalition and SCC should not be allowed to obscure the strong support that SCC enjoyed upon the campus among students who would not themselves join in occupying the buildings. For example, on Friday evening, a group of leaders in the Columbia University Student Council issued a statement calling upon the University to grant amnesty, abandon the gym, abandon IDA, rescind the ban on indoor demonstrations, and to remit the policy-making power of the University to a committee of students and faculty. Since these recommendations virtually coincided with the six demands of the strikers, they give the lie to assertions that "responsible" student opinion disavowed the movement's objectives. The signers included former members of the

Committee on Student Life selected by President Kirk. The Columbia *Spectator's* editorials and commentaries became increasingly favorable to the demonstrators and critical of the Administration. On Sunday evening several hundred students assembled at the Sundial to manifest support for the demonstrators. They vowed to remain until amnesty was granted. The group increased in size throughout the night. Its presence must have buoyed the spirit of SCC and reinforced resistance to compromise.

There is no accurate way to judge the balance of opinion among faculty or students. Sentiment split differently on different issues. The best guide is a poll taken by the Van Am and the Ted Kremer Service Societies on Thursday and Friday. We select three key issues:

1. "I favor amnesty for all students involved in the demonstrations of the last three days"

> YES: 2054 or 37 percent
> NO: 3466 or 63 percent

2. "End gym construction"

> YES: 4093 or 74 percent
> NO: 1433 or 26 percent

3. "End University ties with I.D.A."

> YES: 3572 or 66 percent
> NO: 1855 or 34 percent

We are told that no students in the buildings took part in the poll. If so, a better picture of total sentiment might be reflected by the addition of 1,000 affirmative votes on each of the issues.

Within the buildings time often passed slowly. Each day was a less exciting day than its predecessor, except for rumor, incidents, and political debate. One witness has given us the following description of the life style that prevailed in Fayerweather as the second day of occupancy drew to a close:

The demonstrators were in good spirits and very highly
organized. Food was plentiful, a first aid station was set
up, a lost and found office, a communications room, a
newsletter was mimeographed. People slept in classroom
buildings and hallways. And always meetings and more
meetings lasting long into the night. Participatory democracy. There was a real community spirit; everything belonged to everybody; the building was "liberated." Girls
—about 40%—were not expected to do the kitchen work
alone, for this was a "liberated" area, and boys had to
help. Couples slept together in public view, nobody cared,
we were "liberated": here was a single commune in which
adult hypocrisies did not apply any longer, where people
shared and shared alike, where democracy decided everything, where people were free of adult values and codes.
Fayerweather was tense, "up tight," but free and in high
spirits.

Outside the buildings it was quieter Saturday but on Sunday and Monday tension returned, and the risk of a violent
battle between as many as 2,000 students increased. AHFG
patrols were maintained at Low Library for the purpose of
preventing the occupants of Low from coming and going at
will. Sunday, shortly after midnight, a handful of students
who had left the building sought to gain reentry. They were
blocked, after some scuffling, by the faculty cordon.

Sunday evening saw a resurgence of student pressure to
end the occupation of the buildings by physical means. A
hundred adherents of the Majority Coalition marched from
South Field to the west side of Low Library. They stationed
themselves in a line outside of the faculty cordon, for the purpose of tightening the restrictions upon what went into the
building. Henceforth, they announced, only necessary medical
supplies and attendants would be allowed. The number and
physical size of the Coalition members on the line assured substantial success.

The Coalition's cordon provoked strong debate at the
AHFG meetings in Philosophy Hall. One of AHFG's notable
contributions had been to deter violence among students. Its
own cordon was probably essential to that role. Allowing

others to replace it as the judges of who or what should enter the building, it was thought, might weaken its position. On the other hand was the risk that interfering with the Coalition's blockade would be interpreted as favoritism toward the strikers, which might provoke a violent reaction on the part of the Coalition.

Shortly after midnight on Monday, AHFG decided not to interfere in any way with the blockade. It evolved an elaborate five point resolution to govern conduct at both the hedge and the ledge. Despite weariness and tension some members retained the humor to see the tragic absurdity of university scholars debating whether a hedge or a ledge was a proper point at which one group of students might block the passage of food to another which had barricaded the center of scholarship.*

At SCC the Coalition's blockade produced a strong reaction. Monday, Low's representatives offered a plan to mobilize the Sundial group to run the blockade and simultaneously block access to the Philosophy Hall headquarters of AHFG. Low argued that such action would "cause the Radical Faculty to dissociate from the Ad Hoc Faculty Group" which, it contended, had "abrogated its 'moral force' in an attempt to play realpolitik." Low wanted thus to put the question squarely to the individual faculty member, "Which side are you on?" Fayerweather suggested that no effort be made to challenge the blockade until the AHFG had been requested to assure access to Low. A majority of eight defeated the plan to besiege Philosophy. The Low Proposal prevailed by a vote of nine to one.

Violence ensued. A column of about 60 people, many black,† circled Low three times, carrying cartons of food and

---

* The debate also occasioned a minor schism in the AHFG ranks; Professor C. Lowell Harriss considered the adopted resolution unduly favorable to the SDS and, with two colleagues, walked out of the meeting. Earlier on Sunday Professor Marvin Harris had also dissociated himself from the AHFG at least temporarily. These are the only two public defections of which we know from the ranks of the consciously pragmatic and multi-ideological AHFG.

† The black participants came from the community and oc-

chanting. As the column passed the west side of Low Library most of the group plunged into the Coalition line. A general brawl followed. Strike supporters tried to throw food up to the ledge, but most of it missed the mark. The column withdrew within five minutes, but during the melee, blood was spilled on both sides.

K. *"The Bust"*

Monday afternoon the police were called. Tuesday, in the small hours of the morning, the police cleared the buildings first, and then the campus.

There was great violence. Given the conditions on the campus, violence was unavoidable. The expectation that the campus would be relatively quiet, a hope shared by police and University officials, proved utterly false; since afternoon everyone had known that the "bust" was imminent. Outside the buildings were hundreds of strike sympathizers, many resentful of the presence of police upon any academic campus. In addition, AHFG members of the faculty had pledged themselves, on Thursday, to "stand before the occupied buildings to prevent forcible entry by police" and, on Sunday, according to one interpretation, to "take all measures within our several consciences to prevent the use of force to vacate these building." It would be surprising if there were not also trouble-makers in the throng.

Our assignment does not include responsibility for determining the extent of the violence and culpable misconduct. Such an inquiry could not be usefully conducted without authority over the police. We have probed into the exact role of the University officials. The facts are discussed below.* Otherwise we content ourselves with the barest summary.

At each of the buildings a University representative directed the occupants to evacuate the premises. Everyone who wished was given ample opportunity to leave. Hamilton Hall

cupied buildings other than Hamilton Hall. There is not the slightest evidence that any black student at Columbia took part or gave moral support.

    * See pp. 162–167.

was cleared without violence. One unit of police went through the tunnels about 2:20 A.M. while another shouldered aside some faculty members and forced open the main door. The black students inside made no resistance. They walked, as directed, in the presence of their legal counsel, through the tunnels under Hamilton Hall out to waiting police buses on Amsterdam Avenue. Eighty-six students were arrested in Hamilton Hall.

Low Library was the next building to be cleared. Police used more force here than at Hamilton Hall in breaking the faculty cordon. Inside, the students had decided to resist passively by linking arms and "going limp" when seized. After asking the group through a bullhorn to walk out willingly, the police began to drag individuals away. Some were clubbed.

At Avery Hall, the police again met resistance and responded with force. A combined force of plainclothesmen and uniformed patrolmen entered the building around three o'clock and dragged or carried out the occupants. There were 42 arrests inside Avery Hall.

About 3:15 A.M. the police approached Fayerweather Hall where students and faculty ringed the entrances. Again using force, the police gained access by the north entrance. Later they secured the south entrance as well. Occupants of Fayerweather had reached no collective decision on resistance. Some cooperated and left the buildings voluntarily. Some went limp; others linked arms. Two hundred and sixty-eight persons were arrested in Fayerweather Hall.

Mathematics was the last police objective. Helmeted officers began work on the barricade at about 3:40 A.M. and entered the building at 4:00 A.M. The students inside had wet the stairs with soap and water to make them hazardous for the police; as the barricade fell, some students also locked arms. Less violence seems to have occurred here than elsewhere. There were 203 arrests.

Neither the police activity nor the violence was limited to the occupied buildings, all of which are north of College Walk. The original plan had called for removing the arrested occupants from the campus through the side gates near each building, but when the police found the numbers much greater than anticipated they brought police vans onto College Walk. When the vans proved provocative, an order to clear South Field was given by unidentified police officers. Unknown to the police, the only exit gates south of College Walk were closed and locked, as had been the case all week in order to limit access to the troubled campus. It seems to have been in this part of the operation that the worst brutality occurred.

Our bare, conclusory account describes neither the violence, nor the emotional storm, nor the physical injuries. Yet the hospital records tell a good deal. Sixteen persons sought treatment at Knickerbocker Hospital; 15 were students and one a patrolman. Knickerbocker's ambulance made more than a dozen round trips. Eighty-seven persons, bringing the total to 103, obtained treatment at St. Luke's. Eight were faculty or staff; 62 were graduate or undergraduate students (including five from Barnard); and 13 were New York City Police. The character of injuries ranged from heavy bruises and scalp lacerations to sprains and severe fright. Two fractures are listed. One student was held at St. Luke's and three were admitted to the Columbia infirmary. The rest were discharged.

The arrest statistics go far to dispel the suggestion that the demonstration was the work of "outside agitators" or a small band of Columbia radicals bent upon revolution. There were 692 arrests in the five buildings. Five hundred and twenty-four, or 75 percent, were Columbia students. At least 25 more, or another 3.6 percent, were Columbia alumni. The others appear to have been mostly students from other universities, but there were a few residents of the neighborhood in buildings other than Hamilton Hall. The following figures give a rough idea of the proportion of the student body involved from different parts of the University.

School or Division	Number of Students	Percentage of its Enrollment
Architecture	250	9.73 percent
College	2750	8.79 "
Barnard	2740	6.01 "
General Studies	3000	2.32 "
Graduate Faculties	4000	1.92 "

The proportion of students arrested from other schools (such as the law school) was less than in the cases listed above.

IV

EFFORTS AT PEACEFUL RESOLUTION OF THE CRISIS

A. *The SDS Demonstration*

Even before the demonstration turned into occupation of buildings, Vice-President Truman sought to defuse the occasion. At the start he offered to meet the demonstrators in McMillin Theatre. Probably, no one supposed their leaders would accept. Certainly, the leaders rejected the idea of reasoned discussion, for they made it a condition of any meeting that the Administration should then and there agree to let the mass meeting conduct a trial of the six IDA demonstrators.

Later, after students had crowded into Hamilton Hall, Dr. Truman offered to meet them in the Wollman Auditorium in Ferris Booth Hall. The students refused, apparently through the informal steering committee, and they then formulated four demands—later raised to six—which they insisted had to be granted before there could be any negotiations:

—end all forms of Columbia's affiliation with IDA

—stop construction of the gymnasium

—amnesty for all demonstrators

—grant a new and open hearing to those disciplined for the earlier IDA demonstration

Could anyone in the Administration have foreseen the events that followed, he might have been more vigorous in pressing alternative proposals upon the students, but it will hardly be suggested that the University officials should, then and there, have unconditionally granted the four demands.

B. *The Negotiations with Hamilton Hall*

Wednesday's negotiations between the Administration and Hamilton Hall were a critical turning point in the entire upheaval.* If they had succeeded, probably order elsewhere would have been easily restored.

We can give no sure explanation of the failure to reach a solution along the lines proposed Wednesday evening following the conference between Borough President Sutton, Senator Patterson, Commissioner Booth, Mr. Gottehrer, and President Kirk and Dr. Truman. The proposals were carefully worked out, and a responsible neutral participant thought that they carried a reasonable basis for settlement. Some participants thought that they were to be put before the students by Borough President Sutton and there may have been misunderstanding about the presentation.

In the evening, the style of the two letters must have played a part. The tone of both was authoritarian. Face-to-face discussion between the President or Vice-President meeting the students as equals seeking to resolve a problem might have been more effective. Probably, the students would have had difficulty in any event in reaching a common decision upon any new course of action. Possibly, reluctance to desert the SDS students and other radicals had some influence. We also understand that Dean Platt's letter was taken more as a threat than a proposal; obviously it did not make the University's best offer. According to this theory, President Kirk's letter then came on top of an irreversible decision, too late to be effective.

But the strongest undercurrent seems to have been lack of confidence in the entire University Administration, based

* See pp. 111–113.

upon the past frustration and experience with Columbia's attitude toward the Harlem community. This distrust bred skepticism of the efficacy of a promise to ask the Trustees to consider the suspension of work on the gymnasium and even 'unjustified disbelief in President Kirk's categorical promises with respect to discipline.

We recount the discussions involving Hamilton Hall separately because the facts dispel a suggestion later made in some circles to the effect that the Administration was discriminating in favor of the black students. On Wednesday and even Thursday, Hamilton Hall was the most pressing problem because it was the source of the greatest danger not merely to Columbia but to the City of New York. There is every reason to suppose that the arrangements proposed on Wednesday afternoon and evening, if accepted in Hamilton Hall, would have been quickly extended to all other students, except those on probation and perhaps those who individually destroyed property or broke into files. The failure to extend the offer is adequately explained by the fact that conversations had taken an entirely different tack by the time attention could be directed to the students in other buildings. Probably, the same assurances of limited punishment would not have been extended to the five or six SDS students already on disciplinary probation, but no one can fairly suggest that there is anything arbitrary or unjust in imposing one penalty on students with clear records and another on students guilty of previous infractions of University rules. If the treatment of the latter is subject to criticism, it is in terms of the prior incident.

This is not to say that the attitude of President Kirk and Dr. Truman toward Mark Rudd and certain other student leaders was always the same as their feelings toward the black students. Those who deliberately substitute offensive vulgarity for the amenities that permit civilized human intercourse can hardly complain if the victims of their abuse fail to respond with affection or respect. They who break into a private office and copy confidential files can hardly expect their aggressions to be ignored, for not even the wildest stretch of imagination can convert breaking into files into a form of political demonstration. But whatever the difference in feeling, there was no discrimination in either the proposals for settlement or the arrangements for the intervention of the police. The discussions that led to peaceful submission at Hamilton Hall were entirely the work of the police, combined with physical circumstance and the style of those inside the buildings.

C. Discussions with the Strike Steering Committee

Although the attention of the Administration was primarily focused on Hamilton Hall for most of Wednesday, individual professors were busy talking to students in Low Library, usually with the encouragement of the Administration, and such conversations went on all through the week. One of the minor lessons to be drawn from the event is that constant talk and numerous intermediaries, both authorized and volunteer, are more likely to be a source of confusion than assistance. We deal in this report only with those contacts that seem to have influenced events or otherwise acquired significance beyond the occasion.

The most important event on Wednesday was the College Faculty's resolution. Paragraph 1 declared that a university is dedicated to rational discourse, while paragraph 2 condemned "obstructive behavior and physical violence," "the use of coercion, and the seizure of Dean Coleman as a hostage," and the "invasion of the President's Office and the rifling of his files." Paragraph 3 resolved that "any differences have to be settled peacefully, and we trust that police action will not be used."

Subsequent developments suggest that a blanket declaration of this character, which seems eminently sensible under the conditions in which it is adopted, can all too easily generate consequences that many of its proponents might later join in regarding as unfortunate after conditions have changed. No one wanted to resort to police action on Wednesday afternoon. By Thursday night the situation was altogether different. There was then much better reason to call the police.

By the following Monday night the situation had changed again. One wonders how many of the faculty members who supported the resolution Wednesday would have voted for it on Thursday night or Monday. Yet in its original form, the resolution must have stiffened the student leaders' resolve and encouraged the belief that the Administration had acted against the express wishes of the Faculty of Columbia College when the police were ultimately called.

Paragraph 5 of the Wednesday resolution of the College Faculty petitioned the University immediately to suspend construction of the gymnasium and then to review the whole matter with a group of community spokesmen designated by the Mayor. The Administration acted with reasonable promptness to implement this request. That very afternoon, President Kirk promised the students in Hamilton Hall that he would bring the resolution before the Trustees, and in the evening he gave assurance of his own favorable recommendation. Under the Charter, a meeting of the Board of Trustees requires at least three days notice. The necessity was often stressed by the Administration, notably at the press conference at three o'clock Thursday afternoon. Later that day, the University officials decided more urgent action was required and secured the assent of a majority without the three days notice. The actual suspension of construction was first announced by Dr. Truman early Thursday morning; both then and in a later statement by the Trustees, the action was said to have been taken "at the request of the Mayor."

Given past events, it is hard to see how much more of substance could have been done in a short space of time. Donors and alumni had become deeply involved. The legal problems attendant upon any effort to unwind the project were exceedingly complex. The financial losses could be large.* But distrust engendered by past mistakes and nourished by

---

* Criticisms of Dr. Truman and other officials for exaggerating the potential damages or giving inconsistent statements are ungenerous. The legal situation was exceedingly complex. The highest potential liability was undoubtedly very large, and the lawyers may well have felt obliged to use that figure. No one could do more than guess at the outcome and any sophisticated listener should have known this.

propaganda impaired the value of these steps. The University officials had been adamant for more than two years in the face of rising opposition; even as they promised reconsideration, their emphasis upon the heavy financial losses and repeated assertions that the gym was "not the real issue" seemed to give evidence that there was no real change of mind.

The manner in which the suspension of work was handled significantly impaired its value as a step to a peaceful solution. At first, the Administration told faculty and students that it would take three days notice to convene a meeing of the Trustees, but within a much shorter time it found ways of arranging the suspension. In truth, there was nothing extra-ordinary about the change of position; it takes a little time to find ways around the formal rules. In an atmosphere of spiraling distrust, however, the inconsistency further under-mined confidence in the Administration's statements.

Similarly, the form of the announcement irritated many students and faculty because the recital that suspension was voted as a courtesy to the Mayor seemed symptomatic of the Trustees' determination to maintain the irrelevance of the student or faculty opposition. We understand the legal and financial importance of the City's asking for a suspension, but that scarcely required the pretense the University was unaware of other events. The Trustees' evident desire not to seem to yield to lawless pressure is likewise understandable, but the cold indifference to student and faculty feelings that the statement unintentionally displayed, coupled with its emphasis upon the temporary character of the interruption, deprived the announcement of much tendency to relax emotion.

D. *The Ad Hoc Faculty Group*

Thursday afternoon and the following night were a time of tragic import. We have already described how the group of faculty members meeting in Philosophy Hall became dis-turbed late Thursday afternoon by what they correctly judged to be the hardening position of the Administration. As the Ad Hoc Faculty Group, they adopted their own resolution concerning the handling of the crisis. That night, AHFG forced the University to cancel its request for police intervention.

Although the Ad Hoc Faculty Group was never a coherent organization, its members, both individually and as a group, were motivated by deep solicitude for their university and acted bravely at risk of serious injury. They realized that the Administration was imprisoned by its past—by its inability to grasp the fact that the gymnasium simply could not be constructed in Morningside Park without participation by activist community leaders, by its failure to comprehend the depth and breadth of the student and faculty support precipitated even as early as Thursday afternoon for the students' position, by the distrust flowing from disregard for earlier committee recommendations, and by lack of sympathy for the students' desire for a greater measure of self-determination. The members of the Ad Hoc Faculty Group were also troubled by the faculty's own past failure to concern itself with university issues and student life; now they would assume the responsibilities they had neglected and also have "a piece of the action." Their appraisal of the dangers of calling upon the police, although probably exaggerated in terms of the situation on Thursday, proved a good deal more realistic than the seeming estimate of the Administration. While miscast as mediators, they perceived the need for mediation. They understood as well as anyone—much better than most people—the extent of the revolt, the reason and justice of some student objectives, and the need for fundamental change.

In retrospect, we are quite clear that AHFG forced the postponement of police intervention without giving adequate weight to the consequences of delay and with very little chance of arranging the students' voluntary withdrawal from the occupied buildings. Earlier, on Wednesday, in the opinion of qualified and impartial observers there had been good reason to hope that the Administration's proposal would be accepted by the students in Hamilton Hall and, if they had withdrawn, perhaps students in the other buildings would have followed. When that possibility failed to eventuate, a number of elements stood in the way of successful negotiations.

One was intransigence on the part of SCC leaders. Some are

reported to have believed that police intervention should be precipitated on the theory that the resulting violence would solidify support for their long range objectives. The tactic had been used successfully in the civil rights movement, not to mention the early stages of revolutions in other countries. Very few student leaders supposed that complex negotiations could be carried on by AHFG as mediators pursuing the manner of international negotiations or labor disputes. The prevailing view was that if any proposal acceptable to the students was forthcoming, it would be advanced by the Administration itself under the pressure of events rather than because of mediation. The best way to get that proposal was thought to be to stand pat until the Administration conceded what it would be. The proper role of the liberal members of the faculty, in the SCC view, was to support the revolt against University officials. They kept the talks going chiefly with the idea of leading AHFG members to join them politically.

The second obstacle to meaningful negotiations was confusion, lack of organization, and divided counsel on every side. We have already called attention to the variations in the positions taken by sundry University officials, which cast doubts on the meaning and bona fides of their proposals. The black students displayed great discipline and restraint but the difficulty of working out any kind of accommodation was greatly increased by their practice of denying leaders power to negotiate for the group while insisting at every step upon full participation of the entire body. The white students in the buildings were ill-equipped for constructive action even if they desired to take it. They had no stable common organization. Although the SDS leaders were skillful propagandists in undermining the Administration and had, on this occasion, raised issues evoking very broad student support, their experience in the difficult process of bridging cleavages and healing conflicts was not relieved even by the kind of theoretical discussion to which they had constantly devoted themselves in studying the tactics of dissent. Given a large and amorphous constituency thrown together in an emotional conflict, the initial, extreme demands inevitably became the only common denominator. The insecure leader of a following that lacks the internal structure of a mature organization cannot talk compromise without risk of repudiation as soon as the cry of "sell out" is raised. Among radical students "incremental gains" is an opprobrious epithet. Black and white students had neither the mutual trust nor machinery for coordinating their positions. Each had different priorities, if not goals; and these tended to produce different tactics. Yet each group was somewhat fearful of opening itself to the charge that it had deserted the other.

AHFG's role seems also to have suffered from inherent defects. Even a well-organized academic faculty can hardly do more in such a crisis than manifest solidarity upon these elementary principles upon which all agree. A group can never mediate effectively. The negotiated adjustment of a crisis requires clean lines of communication, central direction, and, on the part of the mediator, the ability to impart and receive confidential communications. For even two or three mediators to work together requires the utmost mutual sensitivity and confidence. AHFG sought to minimize the difficulty by appointing a small number of negotiators, but even the necessity of reporting to a large group presents the actual intermediary with a disastrous dilemma: shall he risk his standing with his own constituency by preserving confidentiality and any slim hope of finding a solution or shall he sacrifice the chance of successful mediation by open disclosure. The active participation of other individuals in talking to the parties, whether as would-be mediators, reporters, or idle conversationalists, multiplies the opportunities for conflict and misunderstanding.

These forces were given free reign at Columbia. They not only added to the confusion, but they also make it clear that many incidents that later created friction among members of the faculty were simply the consequence of too many well-intentioned people seeking to salvage a situation that could be saved, if at all, only by confidential discussions skillfully conducted and tightly controlled by a few individuals.

The notion that AHFG could combine the creation of a third political force on the campus with active mediation was a basically unsound conception. It was bound to offer allies to the rebel students and encouraged them to believe that by further politicizing the faculty they might gain, if not complete victory, at least amnesty, power, and some of their substantive goals. By appearing as allies of the students, the group appeared disloyal to the Administration.

Furthermore, AHFG's own political objectives destroyed any slight hope that it mediate effectively. Disinterestedness was an indispensable qualification. Subjectively, the political goals of sundry AHFG members were bound to shape their attitudes toward the negotiations where a true mediator would have concentrated upon finding the solution most likely to be acceptable to parties. Externally, the credibility of the AHFG representatives as mediators was bound to be impaired by the general awareness that AHFG had its own political goals in the controversy. Thus, students associated with SCC viewed the representations of AHFG spokesmen with distrust because they viewed acts, actually motivated by the desire to avoid a University catastrophe, as selfish bids for power. Knowing that AHFG embraced many diverse elements and voted by a majority of whoever happened to be in the room at any time of day or night, student radicals concentrated their efforts not on the mediation but on further politicizing the faculty with the aid of the AHFG members who were pursuing the students' objectives.

It may have been this basic confusion of role that led AHFG publicly to emphasize from the beginning its own public prescriptions for settlement, which it proposed to support by granting or withholding physical intervention in opposition to the lawfully constituted authorities, instead of concentrating upon quietly bringing the principals to a better appreciation of the essential elements of the situation.

In retrospect, therefore, the intervention of the Ad Hoc Faculty Group, despite its gallantry and high motivation, appears to have had unfortunate consequences. Its initial proffer of a faculty strike and threats of physical intervention to bar the entry of police lent an air of legitimacy to the students' use of physical power as a way of influencing University policy and administration.* The delay of police intervention from

---

* It was the feeling of those who pledged a faculty strike and threatened to obstruct police action by physical interference that these declarations were justified by the need to adopt heroic measures in order to increase the students' faith in their mediation.

Friday to Tuesday at AHFG's request increased the risk of violence and the shock of the Administration's decision to call the police. Although some of the participants believe that the result would have been the same at any time after the students established their internal lines of communication, we are persuaded that the delay strengthened many students' belief that persistent intransigence would succeed and allowed them to convince themselves, by self-sustaining assertion, of the "legitimacy" of their revolution. By Monday night there were more people in the buildings and on the campus. There was more intransigence and more emotion. All these elements increased the ultimate violence. When and whether to call the police to evict hundreds of students were exceedingly difficult questions upon which honest and reasonable men could differ, yet the AHFG resolutions were cast in terms that encouraged the belief that the Trustees and Administration would be guilty of a serious moral wrong if they called for police eviction of student trespassers who forcibly disrupted the University.

Yet perhaps AHFG had no alternative but to make some effort at peaceful settlement despite the great costs of delay. Those who led the group, as we have said, had a much truer understanding of the issues and nature of the conflict than any revealed by the Administration or Trustees. Calling the police to evict hundreds of students could lead only to catastrophe, whether the action came early or late. The effort to avoid catastrophe would have value even though it failed. In our estimation, the most unfortunate consequence of AHFG intervention was that its activities unintentionally added to the moral and political confusion in which the police were called. Perhaps that is the inevitable consequence of the voluntary active participation of a third force in the immediate management of such a crisis, especially in the form of a large and amorphous body which can act only by adopting resolutions, the debate on which invites its own efforts at political manipulation. The proper formal or public role of the faculty or faculty groups in such a crisis may be first, to support the reestablishment of the rule of reason and civility and, second, to make it plain that the Faculty will insist, through those processes, upon prompt reform. A university faculty's ability thus to work its will is beyond question. We are glad to note that the Faculty of

Columbia University is actively pressing the latter role, partly under the leadership of the old Ad Hoc Faculty Group.

On Tuesday, April 30, in the small hours of the morning, following police intervention and harrowing violence, the AHFG Steering Committee drew up a long statement for consideration by the full Ad Hoc Faculty Group. The statement criticized the structure of the University as archaic and many of its policies as insensitive to contemporary political and social reality. It,

> first of all condemn[ed] the persistent unwillingness of the Trustees and Administration to make a rapid and fundamental reevaluation of the moral ambiguities of their position.

The draft resolution then blamed the Administration for failing to persuade the Trustees and asserted that the failure "necessarily means that they will receive a vote of no confidence from the faculty and students." It demanded a faculty fact-finding commission with the particulra assignments of investigating the position of the Trustees and reviewing the role of senior administrators in the crisis. One passage read:

> In the present situation . . . the student leaders are properly calling for a campus-wide strike. In response to last night's events, we believe we are fully within our professional responsibilities in urging our colleagues to respect this strike.

The draft concluded by urging "that there be no irregular occupancy of buildings so that there can be an early return to a policeless campus." The tone of the proposed report was highly political. The University officials, despite indecisiveness and inept public pronouncements, had been considerably more accommodating than the striking students even on the matter of discipline. Yet the proposed AHFG statement laid the blame almost entirely on the Trustees and the Administration. Adoption of the draft would have driven another wedge between warring camps deep into Columbia University. It abandoned all sense of neutrality and seemingly sought to throw the support of the faculty on the side of revolution.

The resolution was presented to the Ad Hoc Faculty Group at a stormy meeting in McMillin Theatre. After several speakers strongly attacked the resolution, Professor Westin, Chairman of the Steering Committee that had prepared the resolution, came to the conclusion that it had been written too hastily under the strain of too much weariness and too strong emotion, and that, since it did not command a firm consensus, its ultimate effect would be only divisive. He, therefore, withdrew the resolution and left the Theatre. The Ad Hoc Faculty Group splintered into dissident factions.

A further word should be added. The efforts of members of the faculty to resolve the crisis brought them into conflict with each other and with the Administration. Some personal wounds were inevitable. We have heard testimony, however, from virtually all the principal participants. It is plain to us that each man acted as he did out of his own deep loyalty to both Columbia and the university ideal.

V

POLICE INTERVENTION

The most difficult problems facing the University during the week of April 23–30 were unquestionably the decisions that had to be made concerning the use of the police. Even through our investigation it was hard and in some cases impossible accurately to establish the relevant facts. The picture contemporaneously available to the Administration when faced with agonizing decisions was inescapably distorted by incomplete information and contradictory reports. For those with the benefit of hindsight, to appraise the decisions reached in a time of stress risks grave injustice to those who had to act under intense pressure during an unprecedented crisis. We have concluded, nevertheless, that we should not dodge the responsibility of comment, since no university can count itself altogether free of the risk of somewhat similar occurrences. There may be something to be learned from the past.

Viewed from the standpoint of police action, there were four critical points in the development of the crisis: April 23, the day when the Sundial demonstration was scheduled; April 24, when the police might first have been used to clear either Hamilton Hall or Low Library or both; the night of April 25–26 when the police were requested to clear the buildings but the request was canceled; and April 29–30 when the use of police to clear the buildings caused violence on a harrowing scale.

A. *Arrangements for April 23*

There were no police arrangements for the Sundial rally, and it is clear that none were required. Rallies of the same kind had been held on campus for a number of years without special police arrangements and, except for the talk of direct challenge to the rule against indoor demonstrations, there was no evidence that this rally would be any different.

There is a strong tradition, not only at Columbia, but in most American universities, that Municipal or State police do not belong on an academic campus. The tradition is recognized by the New York Police Department whose top officials advised us that they would not send policemen onto the campus except at the request of the highest University officials. Columbia University has a security force to protect its property but no police with the broader functions assigned by some universities. Thus, the New York Police Department, although aware of the plan for the Sundial rally, did not have men stationed on campus at the time of the rally. There was one patrolman stationed just off the campus at each end of College Walk, and a squad of ten patrolmen and one sergeant was assigned to the Morningside area in case any trouble developed. It was this squad that went to the gym site when the demonstrators began to tear down the fence. Once the demonstrators returned to the campus, police involvement temporarily ended.

We are equally clear that the right course was followed on Tuesday afternoon, April 23, when the Administration decided not to ask the police to clear Hamilton Hall.

Around 3 P.M. the police received a report that a Columbia dean was being held against his will. Deputy Chief Inspector James Taylor of Patrol Borough Manhattan North called Captain DeNisco, the head of the Campus Security Force, and inquired about the situation. Captain DeNisco advised him that he had personally been in Hamilton Hall and that there was no need for any police action.

Dean Coleman described his perception of the situation as follows:

I doubted seriously how much this would last through the night, and I was of the opinion things would have worked out sufficiently so that I would be able to leave the office.

There was no reason for President Kirk or Dr. Truman to disagree with this estimate. In addition, the building was open and classes were being held. Previous Columbia campus sit-ins had ended without police intervention. The tradition against bringing police onto a university campus was also a restraining influence, although it must be clear that that tradition has little relevance in the case of forcible occupation of university buildings.

B. Wednesday, April 24

By Wednesday morning the situation had changed dramatically. The black students had asked the white students to leave, and then barricaded the doors of Hamilton Hall. Dean Coleman was being held against his will.* There were reports of the introduction of weapons. Outsiders from Harlem and civil rights organizations had entered the buildings. In addition, a large number of white students had broken into Low Library and many of them had gone upstairs to break into and occupy the suite used by President Kirk and other high University officials.

On Wednesday too, however, the Administration refrained from calling upon the police to clear the buildings.

So far as Hamilton Hall is concerned, that decision seems beyond criticism. Shortly after the blacks ejected the white students from Hamilton Hall, Captain DeNisco notified the police. The police immediately sent a squad of about 15 men to the area. By 8 A.M. 35 men had arrived at the campus. Between 8 and 9 A.M., Assistant Chief Inspector Eldridge Waithe and Deputy Chief Inspector James Taylor arrived at Low Library to discuss the situation with President Kirk, Dr. Truman, and other Administration officials.

The immediate problem was to determine what action

_____
* See pp. 103–105.

could be taken to free Dean Coleman. The police officers indicated that it might be possible to pull the grate off the outer window with a hydraulic jack quickly enough for the Dean and his associates to escape. Yet there was risk the effort might provoke reaction from the people in Hamilton Hall and the prisoners might be hurt before the rescue was completed. In addition, Administration officials had talked to Dean Coleman by telephone and he thought he faced no immediate danger. The plan was rejected and Dean Coleman was released about three o'clock that afternoon.

To have called upon the police to evict the students from Hamilton Hall on Wednesday morning would have risked a major riot, affecting the Harlem community. Only a few weeks had passed since the assassination of Dr. Martin Luther King, Jr. In the interval, other cities had experienced major disturbances. No one can accurately estimate the exact degree of the risk but knowledgeable persons from the Harlem community as well as City officials considered it substantial. Apart from all else, that risk could not wisely be undertaken unless there was no other solution. On Wednesday afternoon, there was still good reason to believe that the Hamilton Hall students might leave on terms acceptable to the Administration.

The historian armed with hindsight will probably wish that the situation at Low Library had been handled differently, although the facts are not entirely clear and the Administration's action is readily understandable. There is good reason to believe that on Wednesday morning the police could have cleared the executive offices in Low Library with little violence and the crisis would never have reached its ultimate proportions. Each day's delay increased the difficulty, the risk of violence, and the emotional trauma of police intervention.

Up to 250 students broke into Low Library about 6 A.M. after leaving Hamilton Hall. Perhaps 150 students went on up to the executive offices. Just about this time the policemen arrived on the campus following Captain DeNisco's call. Word of the detachment's arrival reached the students in Low Library, and all but 27 demonstrators fled through the windows, including Mark Rudd. Recollections of the events here begin to diverge, but it seems fairly clear that about this time three things happened: (a) security guards were permitted to enter the suite and remove valuable works of art; (b) the police entered Dr. Kirk's office and possibly others; and (c) the students left Dr. Kirk's office although they remained in some others.

Focusing upon Low Library exclusively, this was clearly the moment to use the police to evict the remaining students, if there was ever to be police intervention.

Dr. Truman testified that the University officials broached this question but were told that the police could not clear Low Library without also moving against Hamilton Hall. He could not recall who spoke for the police but felt sure that the spokesman was an inspector if not a higher official. The University did not press the suggestion further.

Inspector Waithe's recollection is somewhat different. A sergeant who had walked through President Kirk's suite early Wednesday morning advised him that the students could probably be removed with little difficulty. Inspector Waithe discussed this possibility with University officials but was told that the University did not want the police to forcibly remove the students because it might be possible to persuade them to leave voluntarily. Inspector Waithe also advised us that his notes indicate that a statement of the kind described by Dr. Truman was made to the University officials by someone under his command but he believes that the discussion occurred sometime later.

There is no basis for preferring one man's recollection over the other. Both are men of integrity. Both were expressing an honest recollection. Although the stated police policy seems unduly rigid as applied to such a situation as existed upon the Columbia campus, there is little doubt that the statement was made and it is just as plausible to suppose that it was made at one time as the other.

Nor is the confusion about the exact facts surprising. On Wednesday morning the presence of 27 students in Low Library must have seemed insignificant compared to the danger to Dean Coleman and the possibility of major disturbances

in Harlem growing out of the situation in Hamilton Hall.
Indeed, it is quite possible that both Dr. Truman and Inspector
Waithe are accurate in their recollection and that in the confusion of that morning different police officers made contradictory statements to different groups of administrators.

C. Night of April 24–25

By Thursday night the top Administration officials were
convinced that the situation had developed to the point where
serious consideration had to be given to calling upon the
police to clear all the buildings. About 10:30 P.M. they reviewed the situation with top Police Department officials,
including First Deputy Police Commissioner John Walsh,
Chief Inspector Sanford Garelick and Deputy Commissioner
Harcourt Dodds, and also Barry Gottehrer from the Mayor's
Office. The decision was taken to have the police clear both
buildings in the small hours of Friday morning when the
fewest people would be about. A little after 1 A.M. as we have
already described,* the decision was reversed under pressure
of the Ad Hoc Faculty Group.

Later events proved the postponement unfortunate because it intensified the difficulties and traumas of the eventual
"bust." Yet the Administration had no choice but to yield to the
importuning of the Ad Hoc Faculty Group. Calling for police
action against students under any circumstances runs against
the academic grain. To push on in the face of opposition from
a vocal and powerful sector of the faculty, which was asking
only for time to negotiate, would have been divisive. The Ad
Hoc Faculty Group was even threatening at least symbolic
physical obstruction, forcing confrontation and arrests. The
responsibility for the intensification of the ultimate catastrophe
caused by the four day delay thus rests upon the Ad Hoc
Faculty Group, except as it is diluted by the Administration's
failures of understanding concerning the causes and extent
of faculty and student dissatisfaction.

* See pp. 122–123.

D. Night of April 29–30

In view of the large scale violence that resulted, the Commission has carefully reviewed the planning for the police action insofar as it involved, or should have involved, University officials. The command arrangements and tactical dispositions are beyond our purview.

The decision to call upon the police was made by President Kirk with the advice of other Administration officials. While he may have consulted individual members, the decision was executive and the Board of Trustees neither made nor directed it.

The planning encompassed the following specific points:

(1) Students would be ordered to leave by a University official using a bullhorn and would be given the opportunity to leave unmolested.

(2) The buildings would be cleared early in the morning when the fewest people would be on campus and much of Harlem would be sleeping.

(3) The police would use overwhelming force so that students who remained in the buildings, outnumbered at least four to one, would find no point in resisting arrest.

(4) Although the police suggested that it might be desirable to clear the campus before emptying the buildings, the Administration stated that it did not want the campus cleared. The police gave assurance they would not bring police vans on to the campus to remove those arrested. The vans were to be parked along the perimeter of the campus.

(5) The Administration made it plain that it wished no unnecessary arrests.

(6) The Administration expressed concern about plainclothesmen. Police officials assured University officials that it was Police Department policy, whenever possible, to use only uniformed men for the actual clearing of a building, but that some nonuniformed men would be present both to assist in handling the arrest procedure and for investigative purposes. Although many plainclothesmen were, in fact, ultimately involved, it is clear that the University had every reason to believe that the number would not be significant.

(7) The Police Department assumed full responsibility for providing medical assistance to anyone injured, since he would be a person then under arrest.

(8) The University officials repeatedly stressed the importance of avoiding violence. The Police Department expressed the belief that the buildings could be cleared without substantial incidence of injury.

Hamilton Hall, unlike the other buildings, was cleared without resistance to the police or incidental violence. There are two explanations:

First, both the black students of Hamilton Hall and the police had a firm and clear-cut understanding, in advance of the operation, that there would be no resistance whatsoever. Inspector Waithe had been in constant touch with the black students, going in and out of the building. The black students had the advice and assistance of two lawyers from civil rights organizations who presumably had some knowledge of similar incidents. In addition, the black students of Hamilton Hall had proven unusual organization and self-discipline.

Second, since the police could enter Hamilton Hall by a tunnel and take out arrested demonstrators by the same route, there was less need for confrontation or opportunity for an unwonted incident outside Hamilton Hall.

These conditions did not exist elsewhere. Only Low Library had a tunnel that seemed practical to use. There had been no conversations between the police and the students in buildings other than Hamilton Hall or between the students and the Administration, about what would happen when the police were called. Columbia's officials, in retrospect, seem to have been too quick to trust the police officials' assurances that there need be little violence. Anyone sentenced to relive the events of April 29–30 would spare no effort to work out such arrangements. Although the number of buildings, mutual distrust, and general chaos would pose extraordinary difficulties in negotiating and executing such arrangements, the risks of violence and personal injury attendant upon massive police action on a university campus are so enormous, in their absence, as to make the effort imperative.

There were three respects in which the planning proved seriously wrong.

First, the number of students in the buildings was grossly underestimated. Since neither the University officials nor the police could gain access to any of the buildings except Hamilton Hall,* it is to some degree understandable that they did not have an accurate estimate of the numbers inside. It seems to us, however, that the Administration's low estimate largely resulted from its inability to see that the seizure of the buildings was not simply the work of a few radicals but, by the end of the week, involved a significant portion of the student body who had become disenchanted with the operation of their university.

Second, the supposition that the operation could be accomplished while the campus was quiet and largely empty proved utterly false. Perhaps it would have some foundation early Friday morning, but by Monday night there was little chance that the necessary preparations could be made and over a thousand police officers could be assembled without word spreading to everyone interested in the events. The campus was constantly covered by radio, television, and newspaper reporters. In fact, everyone had virtually certain knowledge that the police were coming on Monday night, and the campus was in crowded turmoil.

Third, both the Administration and the police mistakenly assumed there would be no opposition to the police outside the buildings. The mistake was related to the erroneous supposition that the campus would be relatively empty but one armed with hindsight can also see that here again the Administration failed to appreciate the extent of support for the demonstrators and of opposition to police intervention on the part of faculty and student, outside the buildings.

The violence and physical injuries can largely be traced to these miscalculations. The violence occurred only after the police had to employ force either to remove faculty and students who were blocking entrance to the buildings or to remove students from the buildings who refused to move after being placed under arrest. The idea that the demonstrators would

---

* Both the police and the Administration had accurate estimates of the number of people in Hamilton Hall.

see the futility of resistance because they were so vastly outnumbered proved irrelevant because the contingent of police
was no more than equal to the total number of people either
in the buildings or blocking the entrances. The presence of
such large numbers of people also made it necessary for the
plainclothesmen who were present to join in the tactical operation. We also understand that the Police Department's
inability to assign the required number of uniformed patrolmen
made it necessary to use many more plainclothesmen than
originally intended.

The extent of the opposition to the police action made it
impossible for them to remove all the students through the
side exits from the campus. This required the police to change
their plans in the middle of the operation and bring police
vans on to College Walk, contrary to the arrangement with
University officials. It was while these vans on College Walk
were being loaded that the police, without consultation with
University officials, determined that they would have to clear
the area around College Walk—again contrary to the original
understanding. The police then attempted to force the students
off South Field without realizing that all the exits at that end
of the campus were locked. At this juncture the worst of the
violence occurred.

The risk of violence, even with the best of planning, is an
inseparable incident of police action against hundreds of
demonstrators. The situation at Columbia on April 29–30 was
plainly different from a sit-in demonstration by 25 or 30 or
even 100 students. Inside and outside the buildings perhaps
2,000 people were involved—700 to 1,000 inside the buildings.
In chaotic conditions, with intense emotions surging through
crowds of rival youths, the degree of risk becomes so high
that it must be taken into account in any decision to invite
police action. The violence and ensuing injuries have had such
disastrous effects upon Columbia in intensifying divisions,
mutual distrust, and self-supporting cycles of fantasy within
insulated factions that one is tempted to conclude that some
other course simply had to be found.

Yet we cannot say that the decision to call in the police was
wrong, once the situation on April 29 had been developed.

Three courses of action were open, and the Administration had to choose one: (a) to call in the police with all possible safe-guards; (b) to grant amnesty, abandon the gymnasium, and concede whatever additional demands were necessary to induce the students to leave voluntarily; or (c) to close the University for an indefinite period, probably until the end of the semester, and hope that order could be maintained despite the rising tension among groups seeking to isolate or recapture the buildings. To talk of further negotiations or other solutions is to ignore the hard choices the Administration had to make; there was virtually no chance of successful negotiations. Furthermore, the third possibility was scarcely feasible; letting things drag along entailed a high degree of risk of serious violence.

It is also wholly unfair, even to the point of disingenuity, for anyone involved in the events of April 29–30 to hold the University officials, or even the University and the police together, solely responsible for the violence and physical injuries. Although the police force may have become excessive, a share of the responsibility for the injuries they inflicted falls upon those students and faculty who, by resisting the police, either actively or passively, made it necessary for the police to use force with the inherent risk that it might easily get out of hand.* This does

---

* Individual statement of Commission member Amsterdam: "One who resists a policeman doubtless ought to be held morally accountable for the policeman's legitimate use of force to overcome his resistance. Events may also very well hold him physically accountable for creating the risk that the police force will get out of hand. I see no moral utility to taxing him, in the realm of conscience, for the policeman's use of excessive and illegitimate force. It seems to me that he may properly expect that the policeman will not use excessive force. The propriety of this expectation is not based upon factual probabilities, but upon a standard of conduct for police which society cannot afford to relax. I would not hold students, faculty or Columbia's administration responsible for police excesses. Notions of joint and several liability seem to me too fine for service here. Their invocation inevitably dilutes responsibility, which ought to be rested squarely on the police in the expectation—enforcible by all the moral force of which we are capable, if by nothing else—that they will live up to it. To this extent, I disagree with the text of our report. I also have trouble

not excuse or even mitigate the blame resting upon the police for using excessive force, nor does it exculpate the Administration of its faults. But we find it difficult to understand how the faculty members, who opposed the Administration's decision to use the police because they feared that violence might result, can justify their own physical intervention the only possible result of which was to increase the chance of violence. They not only required the police to use force against them but they thus encouraged those occupying the buildings to offer forcible resistance. A better way to minimize the possibility of violence, might have been to go to the buildings as observers and to have endeavored to convince the students both within and without the buildings not to resist policemen carrying out the orders of the Administration.

---

with the slippery notion of 'passively resisting' a police officer, a phrase whose meaning usually and here is at best obscure and at worst logically impossible."

VI

THE DISTURBANCES OF MAY 22–23, 1968

The police action on the night of April 29–30 cleared the buildings and brought a degree of peace to the campus, but the University did not settle back to normal routine. For a month a student strike disrupted normal University classes, except at certain professional schools. Then, on May 22, another bloody engagement occurred between students and police.

Since the second "bust" took place after the Fact-Finding Commission had been established, it falls outside the literal charter given to the Commission by the Executive Committee of the Faculty. We were nevertheless of the unanimous opinion that discussion of the causes of the second outbreak is fairly comprehended within the spirit of our instructions because it was, in a substantial sense, an integral part of the original disturbances.

A. *The Events*

Background. The police "bust" on the night of April 29–30 aroused intense emotion. Immediately, a students' Strike Co-ordinating Committee (SCC) composed of representatives from numerous established and spontaneously-formed student organizations organized a University-wide strike. The extent of the support for the strike was hotly disputed but, except at cer-

tain professional schools, it was enough to disrupt normal educational activities. Probably, the strike had the support of a
great majority of the students outside the professional schools.
Several hundred faculty members gave some form of support.
One hundred twenty-five members of the rump AHFG group,
for example, voted to respect the strike by cancelling classes.
Others refused to uphold a strike as such but elected to meet
with their classes on campus lawns or away from University
property in order to express their condemnation of the Administration's use of police. By May 2, 340 faculty members
had signed a petition backing the strike.

In the ensuing days, the police were withdrawn from the
campus. The Fact-Finding Commission on the Columbia Disturbances, the Faculty Executive Committee, and the new stu-
dent-Trustee (Temple) Committee were established. Classes
and libraries were picketed by a few students. Many more
attended daily rallies at the Sundial. The professional schools
returned to rather normal operations by the end of the first
week of May. On May 9, a brief scuffle broke out in front of
Low Library when a group of "jocks" tried to seize the ampli-
fying equipment being used by "pukes" at their outdoor rallies.
Pickets also appeared in front of the homes of a number of
Columbia trustees. SCC broke up during the third week of
May when a relatively moderate group chiefly concerned with
the issue of structural reform at Columbia established itself as
the Students for a Restructured University (SRU). The rup-
ture was precipitated by Mark Rudd's appearance at Junior
High School 271 in the Brownsville section of Brooklyn. His
wide-ranging appearances at many protests and demonstrations
throughout New York antagonized the students whose chief
concern was University reform. The new group was also irritated by the domineering tactics of SDS leaders who, for all
their reference to the theme of "participatory democracy," refused to admit any ideas but their own.

The prevailing emotion and disorder were reflected in a
serious incident on the evening of May 17. A rally sponsored
by the Community Action Committee was held at 8 P.M. to
condemn the University's eviction of tenants residing in Colum-
bia-owned buildings. Michael Golash, an engineering student

who was the committee's leader, demanded the return of all University-owned buildings to the community. Golash, Mark Rudd, and others then led over 400 marchers to a building just off the campus. Most of the protesters sat down in front of the former apartment house. A few went inside. At 4 A.M. on May 18, a police contingent commanded by Assistant Chief Inspector Eldridge Waithe cleared the building without violence. Fifty-six of the 117 persons arrested were Columbia students. None of them had been "busted" on April 30.

Disciplinary procedure. In the midst of these discordant and confused circumstances the Administration initiated disciplinary proceedings against participants in the disturbances of April 23–30. The step revived the unresolved conflict between the demonstrators' demand for total amnesty and the Administration's insistence upon disciplinary measures the final authority for which would be vested in President Kirk alone. Clearing the buildings brought no resolution of the issue. Amnesty simply became a demand of the striking students.

During the week of April 23–30, it will be recalled, the Galanter-Hovde-Trilling Committee had drawn up a plan for a Tripartite Joint Committee on Disciplinary Affairs made up of equal numbers of representatives of student, faculty, and Administration representatives. The plan was accepted, in principle, as part of a broader resolution adopted at the Sunday meeting of the Faculties on Morningside Heights.* That afternoon the three professors formally submitted to the President written recommendations for the composition, jurisdiction, and procedures of the Joint Committee on Discipline, including the names of the persons to serve. On the most controversial issue the report seems a bit ambiguous, for it stated both that the decisions of the Joint Committee would be binding and that it recognized the "statutory responsibilities of the President." The intent was undoubtedly to provide the substance of finality, even though form was left obscure. President Kirk approved the recommendation on Monday and announced that he would ask the Board of Trustees to reexamine University statutes on disciplinary matters in the light of recommendations

---

* See pp. 128–133.

made by the new Joint Committee. For the present, however, the ultimate judicial authority was left in President Kirk's hands.

The Joint Committee on Discipline convened on May 3. On May 9, it issued recommendations dealing with "the particular disciplinary measures to be taken with regard to participants in the demonstrations and to the general procedures that should be followed in this case."

The first part of the recommendations dealt with the substantive offenses and their punishment. The key points were—

> Voluntary participation in the demonstrations asserted a common responsibility for their consequences. Therefore, a uniform discipline should be imposed for the act of participation as such.

> All participants in the demonstration should be placed upon disciplinary probation through June 30, 1969.

>   *   *   *   *

> The demonstrators as a group should not be held responsible for malicious acts of individuals, but those individuals cannot be allowed to escape the consequences of their personal acts.

> In the light of these initial conclusions, the Dean of each School or Faculty should determine which students in that School or Faculty were involved in the demonstrations and, following discussions with those students, should impose the discipline recommended above. A student who fails to appear before the Dean should be suspended. If the student believes that the penalty imposed upon him by the Dean is excessive in view of that recommendation, he may appeal directly to the Joint Committee on Disciplinary Affairs.

The second part of the recommendations dealt with the procedure to be followed in the case of students who denied participation in the disturbances or were charged with some more serious offense. Here it is sufficient to say that the procedure provided for a hearing before a school tribunal composed of

two members of the faculty, two students, and one adminis-
trator, with other safeguards of procedural due process. Appeals
could be taken to the Joint Committee. On the vexed issue of
the finality of its decisions, the Joint Committee proposed:

> The President of the University, on further review of the
> proceedings, may take such revisions in the decisions of the
> Joint Committee as he believes to be in the best interests
> of the University. The President and the Trustees should
> agree that the President will *not increase* the penalty which
> has been sustained or imposed by the Joint Committee.
> (Italics added.)

Underlying both the substantive and procedural recommendations was the plainly-stated predicate:

> These recommendations are predicated on the assumption
> that trespass charges will be dropped.

We find no merit in the suggestion that the pendency of
criminal charges logically and automatically bars academic
discipline until their final disposition. If that rigid rule were
sound, it would be equally applicable to potential criminal
charges and no university discipline would be possible until
the expiration of the period of limitations. Countless organizations must deal with the various internal problems resulting
from misconduct of their employees, members, or associates,
even though the same misconduct is a public offense: for
example, employers, labor unions, clubs, political parties, and
academic institutions.

But although no abstract principle raises a barrier, practical
considerations of fairness may call for staying private action.
We think that the plainly stated predicate underlying the
recommendations of the Joint Committee on Discipline had
prime importance. To proceed with academic discipline while
criminal charges were pending would not only have invited
obfuscating propaganda but it would also have raised several
serious issues. Any students charged before two tribunals
could argue—at least with superficial plausibility if not with
real hope of success—that their constitutional rights were violated because they were being put in jeopardy twice for the

same offense. More serious would be the problem of determining what academic punishment was appropriate for one who might still be sentenced by the criminal court. The very conduct of an academic proceeding against a student charged with criminal trespass could complicate his defense in either the academic forum or the criminal court. Full disclosure might well be the best response to any academic charges, but admissions made in the academic proceeding would, as a matter of law, be competent evidence against a student in the criminal prosecution. Disclosures concerning the defense might be prejudicial. A finding of guilt might influence the prosecutor's exercise of discretion, and even the rulings of the trial court. Some of these problems—perhaps all—could be solved by imaginative procedure and careful attention to the substantial rights of the student, but they emphasize the wisdom of the Joint Committee's basic hypothesis.

Unfortunately, the Administration rejected both the Joint Committee's hypothesis and its recommendation that the President agree not to increase any penalties imposed by the Joint Committee. On the same day that he received the recommendations President Kirk "commended" the committee for the "promptness" of its report and accepted its recommendations "except for two reservations and two principal comments."

The comments consisted, first, of the observation that "it is imperative that these disciplinary procedures move swiftly" and, second, of the caveat that the proposed procedures should not bind any Dean.

The reservations, as stated above, were, first, a categorical refusal to surrender the ultimate power to increase as well as decrease punishment and, second, a statement that the University would not drop the criminal charges.

> However, the trespass charges cannot be dropped by the University. A criminal charge, once lodged, is also in the hands of the public prosecutor representing the people of the State of New York and of the judge before whom the charges are brought. Furthermore, I am advised that, under the Code of Criminal Procedure, crimes committed riotously may not be compromised.

The quoted words, read literally, are technically accurate. But the statement omits another truth—that the University, if it wished, had ample power to express its desire not to press the simple trespass charges and to ask the public prosecutor and the judge that they be dismissed. Indeed, the University has now taken that very step.

President Kirk's statement put the Joint Committee in a dilemma: it must either stand its ground—which would have meant publicly attacking the President, destroying the tripartite procedure so laboriously constructed, and washing its hands of the whole affair—or else it must accept his reservations despite the ill-will and procedural tangles that the reservations might generate.

The Joint Committee strove for a middle course. On the issue of Presidential review, it elicited a statement that, in the unlikely event that President Kirk disagreed with an appellate decision of the Joint Committee, he would submit the matter to a distinguished alumnus for final decision. On the concurrent criminal charges, the Joint Committee proposed to avoid at least some of the problems by suspending the execution of any academic punishment until after their disposition:

> The Joint Committee suggests that Deans begin to implement its recommendations concerning intramural discipline, but that application of all penalties be held in abeyance, pending action in the courts. The Joint Committee will entertain an appeal from a penalty applied before the final disposition of trespass charges against a student, even if that penalty is otherwise consistent with the Joint Committee's recommendations.

The step did nothing, however, to minimize any prejudice that might result from forcing a student to meet academic charges while criminal proceedings were pending against him.

The new plan was announced in a statement issued by the Joint Committee on May 13, 1968. The statement emphasized the right of any student to appeal the Dean's decision if any penalty whatever was applied to him before final disposition of criminal trespass charges. It also renewed the explicit warning that a student who failed to appear before a Dean was liable to immediate suspension even though a trespass charge was pending against him.

On May 16, 1968, the Dean of Columbia College sent identical, registered letters to Mark Rudd, Nick Freudenberg, Morris Grossner, Ed Hyman, and Ted Gold summoning them to the Dean's office on Tuesday afternoon, May 21, no later than 5 P.M. The entire letter read:

> You are charged with participating in the recent demonstrations starting on April 23, 1968 and are requested to come in to see me on Tuesday afternoon, May 21, no later than 5:00 P.M. In accordance with the recommendation of the Joint Committee on Disciplinary Affairs, I should inform you that if you fail to come in to see me by the above date, you shall be suspended from the University.*

These five students were selected by the Dean's office upon the instructions of President Kirk. All five were prominent SDS leaders. All five were already on probabtion as a result of the IDA demonstration on March 27, so that their punishment for participating in the April disturbances might be more severe than the disciplinary probation to which the general group of participants was subject under the Joint Committee rule. The reason for selecting the five may or may not have been the fact that they were on probation. So far as the record before us reveals, no other students suspected of participating in the April disturbances were already on probation when the disturbances occurred.

A day or two later the Dean of Columbia College also summoned a number of seniors to his office charging them with participation in the April disturbances.

The four SDS students summoned to the Dean's office immediately announced that, when the time came, they would refuse to appear. Their lawyers are reported to have advised them that appearing before the Dean's representative would

---

* Apparently Mr. Gold never received the letter addressed to him, but letters addressed to Messrs. Rudd, Freudenberg, Grossner and Hyman were duly received.

risk double jeopardy and self-incrimination. Attorneys of the New York Civil Liberties Union and the National Lawyers' Guild demanded postponement of the academic proceedings until the criminal charges had been disposed of. An action was instituted in the United States District Court seeking to enjoin the academic proceedings.* Sometime prior to the afternoon of May 21, Dean Platt encountered on the campus three or four of the SDS students summoned to his office. They told him that they would refuse to appear. He explained to them that their appearance could not prejudice their defense of either the academic or the criminal charges because its only purpose was to determine whether they wished to admit guilt, deny the charges, or stand silent; standing silent would be treated as a denial. Later, the students' oral statement that they would not appear was confirmed by a telegram sent to Dean Platt by their lawyers. Thus the stage was set and the script written for another confrontation.

At 4 P.M. on the afternoon of May 21—an hour before the deadline—SDS held another rally at the Sundial. Mark Rudd told the crowd that he could not see the usefulness of talks over disciplinary action "when the University wants to expel us, no matter what." About 350 students and sympathizers then followed three lawyers and about 20 parents into Hamilton Hall. Dean Platt, who had been watching the rally, sent word that he would meet with the four students or their lawyers on South Field, but not in his office; he was reluctant to let the demonstration concentrate on the confined area of Hamilton Hall. His offer was rejected.

Around 5 P.M. Dean Platt returned to his office. The four students had not appeared. Under the Joint Committee's two statements and the Dean's letter, non-appearance brought automatic suspension, not because of a finding of guilt upon the charges but because failure to respond to the Dean's summons was itself an offense. When Dean Platt entered Hamilton Hall, he was confronted by the lawyers, parents and student protesters all demanding that the suspensions be

---

* Some weeks later Judge Marvin E. Frankel entered an order denying a preliminary injunction.

held in abeyance. Dean Platt agreed to meet with the lawyers in his office, while the concerned parents waited in an adjoining room. The lawyers asked to stand in the students' place. Dean Platt rejected the request. Then, since the lawyers were not familiar with their contents, Dean Platt explained to them the substance of the two Joint Committee memoranda on discipline; he also pointed out that the students could stand mute when they came in. All questions of a legal nature the Dean referred to University counsel. One attorney then asked for a one-day extension of proceedings. Dean Platt refused; his instructions from his superiors, as he understood them, gave him no discretion. The lawyers left.

About 6 P.M. Dean Platt met with the parents in his outer office. There was heated discussion of the proposed suspensions. Toward the end of the meeting, the parents' spokesmen requested a second meeting the following morning to continue the discussion. Dean Platt went into the inner office and called Dean Coleman who agreed to meet with the parents at 9 A.M. He then stepped outside his office, announced that, "The parents will meet with Dean Coleman at 9 A.M.," and left the building. Immediately after the Dean's departure one parent told the group, "We are meeting to discuss the question of holding the suspensions in abeyance." In fact, the suspensions were made effective as of 5 P.M.

The confusion gave rise to a controversy that no one can resolve. The parents interpreted Dean Platt's remarks to mean disciplinary action would be postponed pending further conversations in the morning. One member of the group told the Commission that Dean Platt had stated, in reply to a specific question, that the 9 A.M. meeting would cover the holding of the suspensions in abeyance. Dean Platt, however, had specifically promised *only* to continue discussion. In the University's view, apparently, the suspensions were, by virtue of the Joint Committee's rules, the necessary and automatic consequence of the four students' refusal to appear. We have no method of establishing exactly what was said on this occasion or of determining how far one side or the other should be blamed for the misunderstanding that arose. The misunderstanding, however, played little part in the course of events.

Summons to the police. While Dean Platt was meeting with
the lawyers and parents, President Kirk, Vice-President Truman, and Dean Coleman were in Low Library discussing the
situation in Hamilton Hall. Apparently, they began to discuss
issuing an ultimatum and calling the police sometime around
5:00 or 5:30 p.m. Dean Coleman testified:

> [We] were discussing the situation that we had another
> sit-in in Hamilton Hall and it was pretty well agreed upon
> by all that we could not allow this to continue again, and
> at this point Columbia had better do what was obviously
> being done now at other institutions that had learned a
> great deal from us, that students would have to be told
> they would have to get out of Hamilton Hall or else we
> would bring police in to clear them out and those arrested
> would be suspended.
>
> This would be . . . announced to them. We did talk
> with Dean Platt over the phone. He asked us to wait until
> he had some sessions with the lawyers and the parents.

When Dean Platt, after talking with the parents, left Hamilton Hall the decision to pursue this course of action had already been taken. Dean Coleman then walked over to Hamilton
Hall and announced over a bullhorn that the students must
leave the building; if they refused, Dean Coleman stated, the
police would be summoned, the students still in the building
would be arrested, and they would be suspended for an indefinite period. Dean Coleman also acknowledged that the four
students who failed to respond to the summons to the Dean's
Office had been suspended. He thereupon left the building.

About 7:40 p.m. Dean Coleman returned to Hamilton Hall
and stated: "As an officer of this University I have no alternative but to call the police. Any student arrested will be suspended for an indefinite period."

More than 200 students disregarded Dean Coleman's order
and stayed in the Hamilton Hall lobby. Police began to assemble near the campus around 8:30 p.m. In mid-evening,
President Kirk held a press conference to announce the University's intention to clear Hamilton Hall. He stated that the
police were requested to treat the demonstrators as gently as

possible. "Our desire," he said, "is to get the building cleared with no violence."

During the evening the students inside the building canvassed the utility of their protest, and many began to think of leaving before the police moved in. A vote was taken around 11 P.M. A slim majority voted to leave the building then and there. The SDS leadership, however, refused to accept the vote as conclusive. Ted Gold went to the balcony of Hamilton to call upon the large crowd outside Hamilton to join the ranks of the protesters. A barrage of speakers arose inside, exhorting the demonstrators to remain. Shortly after midnight a new vote was taken. One hundred favored staying, 80 voted to leave and 30 abstained. One leader rose to continue the debate. Mark Rudd cut him off: "I'm sorry, the decision has been made."

Mr. Rudd also appears to have frustrated a responsible effort to clear the building without police action. Professors Terrence Hopkins and William Reinmuth, in the company of some colleagues and SDS leaders, drew up a five point plan for presentation to both the Administration and the students in Hamilton Hall. Recollections about the details were imprecise by the time of our investigation but the proposal apparently contemplated:

1) a recital that the appearance in the Dean's office was required merely to inform students of the charges,
2) that no discipline by reason of the disturbances should bar a student's graduation,
3) that no academic discipline should be imposed pending the criminal charges,
4) that the suspensions of Messrs. Rudd, Freudenberg, Grossner and Hyman should terminate when they did appear before a Dean, and
5) that if the students left the building, they would be suspended but no police action would be taken.

The proposal was brought to Dr. Truman in Low Library. He replied that he did not have the power to negotiate but would hold the question open until he heard more of the acceptability of the plan to the students. The SDS leaders who

had participated in framing the proposal took it to Mark Rudd
and other leaders in Hamilton Hall. Mr. Rudd categorically
rejected the plan. When it was put before the demonstrators
for a vote, he condemned it as an Administration trick. The
students rejected it.

At 12:45 A.M. on May 22, some 75 demonstrators voluntarily
left the building. At 2:30 A.M., City police, under the direction
of Chief Inspector Sanford Garelick, entered Hamilton Hall
by the underground tunnels. The demonstrators were arrested
and taken from the building without violence.

Clearing the campus. Unhappily, the absence of violence
inside Hamilton Hall stands in strange contrast to the violence,
provocation and brutality that soon ran rampant outside the
building. Earlier in the evening the news that President Kirk
had called for police intervention, coupled with the build up
of police forces near the campus, evoked a bitter and hostile
response. Recollections of the night of April 29–30 were too
fresh to view renewed police action without emotion. After
midnight, as the time for the police action approached, tension
rose. Shortly before 2 A.M. a group of plainclothesmen was
spotted and chased from campus. A WKCR reporter was
blackjacked. The mood turned angry, and then hostile. Vast
numbers of students milled around campus. Groups formed at
each end of Campus Walk and began to barricade the entrances
to Amsterdam Avenue and Broadway, using wooden police
"horses," large aluminum sheets, and trash barrels. While the
evacuation of the demonstrators was underway, two small
fires broke out in Hamilton Hall. A larger fire broke out in
Fayerweather Hall, which took about forty minutes to contain.
At this time, too, the research papers of Professor Orest
Ranum were burned on the sixth floor of Hamilton Hall.

Despite the buildup of tension, there was evidently some
reason to think that the crowd would quiet down following the
removal of the demonstrators. Dean Platt, who had been all
over the campus, felt the chances were good. He went to Low
Library to inform President Kirk of his conclusion and was told
that the decision had already been made to bring in the police.
The decision was President Kirk's. The reports of the fires in
Hamilton and Fayerweather Halls, as well as breakage of

windows and doors, the throwing of eggs and bricks, and the erection of barricades convinced him that the disturbances were getting out of hand.

The record leaves grave uncertainty concerning the arrangements with the police. Dr. Truman testified:

> We specifically suggested to Chief Inspector Sanford Garelick the possibility that if he were simply to form a line there, at the north edge of South Field, and not attempt to do anything more than that—but leave South Field as a more or less free area—that this would avoid any further the kind of incidents that had occurred. And he assented to that.

But at 4:05 A.M. President Kirk had read over WKCR an announcement which is at direct variance with Dr. Truman's testimony:

> The police have been requested by the University to clear all campus academic buildings. The police have also been requested to clear the campus of all persons under penalty of arrest. Dormitory residents are to remain in their rooms. All other persons, including dormitory residents not in their rooms, must leave the campus immediately via the nearest campus gate.

Aware that the President's order could not be heard by the students outside the buildings, Dean Platt rushed back to the Sundial and, about 4:20 A.M., he told 800 to 1,000 students of the decision through a bullhorn; he pleaded that they return to their dormitory rooms.

The police came. Hell broke loose. One hundred students locked arms behind the barricades at Amsterdam Avenue. Hundreds more crowded close to the gate. The police swiftly dismantled the obstruction. The hundred broke and ran. But 2,000 students live in dormitories facing South Field. Many of them and hundreds of other persons were crowded on the campus. For most, the character of the police action was a profound shock; neither they nor others in the Columbia community appreciated the extent of the violence which is the probable concomitant of massive police action against hun-

dreds, if not thousands, of angry students. As the police advanced, most students fled. Whether they had a fair chance to
return to their rooms is a matter of dispute. Some police first
warned the students; others chased and clubbed them in-
discriminately. But not all students went to their dormitories
and some who fled came back out to attack the police. Bottles
and bricks were hurled by students. A number of police were
injured. The action grew fiercer. The battle see-sawed two or
three times between the South Field and the entrances to the
dormitories, then 50 plainclothesmen and non-uniformed police
came onto the campus. They charged into Livingston and
Hartley Halls, clubs swinging. In Furnald Hall they chased
and clubbed students as high as the fourth floor landings. By
5.30 A.M. the campus was secured.

Although we have neither pursued the details nor sought
to reconstruct the bloody affray, two conclusions are beyond
dispute. First, the police engaged in acts of individual and
group brutality for which a layman can see no justification
unless it be that the way to restore order in a riot is to terrorize
civilians. Dean Platt testified that when he pointed out to two
police officers the brutal charge of the plainclothesmen in front
of Furnald Hall, the officers replied that they could see no
policemen. Second, some students attacked the police and
otherwise provoked the retaliation. Their fault was in no way
commensurate with the brutality of the police and, for the
most part, was its consequence. But some students' conduct
shocked and repelled even some of the radicals who had
occupied the buildings during April 23–30.

B. Appraisal

The affair of May 21–22 was a phase of the confrontation
that began on April 23. Clearing the buildings on the night of
April 29–30 had done nothing to resolve the crisis. The issues
remained. The antagonisms were deepened. There was quiet
but not the usual order. The outbreak of further turbulence
should not have been surprising.

The immediate cause was the mutual desire of the Administration and SDS for a further confrontation. The Administration gave every sign of insistence upon promptly and vigorously punishing leaders of the April uprising even while the campus was in a state of high, continuing tension. And at least some SDS students were apparently more than willing to escalate the action.

Reasonable men will reach different judgments about the wisdom of pressing campus discipline against the four SDS leaders while the University was still in turmoil. Since they were the same students whose punishment for the IDA demonstration on March 27 had been a major issue in the demonstrations of April 23–30—an issue on which the Administration was not beyond criticism—prosecuting new charges at that time obviously carried a very high risk of further demonstrations, of need for police action, and of ensuing violence. But even if that risk had to be taken, proceeding while the criminal charges were pending offered an unnecessarily vulnerable target because it could readily be made to appear—and perhaps could have been—unfair to the accused.

The confrontation itself could have been postponed or even avoided, without prejudice to anyone, if both the Administration and the four students had sought to avoid it with even a modicum of skill. The letters summoning Messrs. Rudd, Freudenberg, Grossner and Hyman gave no explanation of what was expected of them when they appeared before the Dean. Nothing informed them whether they were merely to plead or whether their guilt would be determined. Nothing told them that they could stand silent. They had no way of knowing the consequences attaching to the several courses of action. Dean Platt's letter did not mention, and apparently did not enclose, the statements issued by the Joint Committee on May 9.

Whatever their true motives, the SDS students acted as if they were looking for confrontation, not clarification. They were advised by counsel. If their only concern were the possible prejudice of dual proceedings, they could easily have appeared in the Dean's office before 5 P.M., asked permission to bring in their lawyers, asked questions, explained the difficulty of their position, and then presented any arguments or requests. An outright refusal to appear was not necessary to protect their legal or practical positions, even if all their legal theories were correct. It was far more consonant with the SCC position that no discipline could be legitimately meted out by the Administration because the Administration itself was illegitimate.

It is clear to us that no student has a right or privilege under any circumstances to ignore a Dean's summons (unless he is disabled by illness or other emergency). Whatever his legal or practical objections, the only proper course is to appear and present them. No rights are waived by such course. No college or university can operate unless unexcused failure to respond to such a letter as Dean Platt's is treated as an infraction of discipline.*

Even though the confrontation on May 21 appears to have been essentially a continuation of the postponed showdown on the question of amnesty, one cannot be sure. Doubt about the meaning of the Dean's summons may possibly have influenced the four students' refusal to appear. They are not to be held to the same clarity to legal analysis as a lawyer subsequently reviewing the events. We cannot tell what advice their lawyers gave them. The lawyers apparently lacked relevant information, because the Dean's office had not drawn the students' attention to the statements of the Joint Committee in any formal fashion. The students' conversations with Dean Platt on campus may or may not have been understood. They may or may not have been repeated to the attorneys. It must be remembered too that the campus was still in a state of confusion and emotional tension in which no one viewed events with the precision that is possible in retrospect. Consequently, while we are entirely clear that the four students were wrong, both technically and substantially, in refusing to appear at the Dean's office, they may have been genuinely concerned about the procedure and, if so, there is something to be said in mitigation of that offense. In this respect, our conclusion is much the same as that of the Joint Committee as expressed in the appeal of AB,† although we might give

---

* Commission member Amsterdam disagrees with this paragraph.

† The text appears as Appendix H, pp. 216–222.

somewhat more weight to the uncertainties with which the four students were confronted. The second critical point in the affair of May 21–22 came when Dean Coleman, upon President Kirk's instructions, ordered the students to leave Hamilton Hall under threat of suspension and police action; and the students refused. The students' refusal was wrong. One group of SDS leaders, with ample time for reflection, produced the decision to stay. They carry responsibility for forcing resort to police assistance with consequent violence.

But there is also room for misgivings about the Administration's decision to order the students from Hamilton Hall, under threat of suspension and police action, as early as 6:30 P.M. For President Kirk to fix the academic penalty for staying, without consultation with the Joint Committee, arguably undercut the Joint Committee principle that guilt and penalties should be determined after a fair hearing with effective student participation. The Joint Committee apparently ratified the decision that those who stayed in Hamilton Hall should be suspended on June 3, 1968, but approval of a presidential decision already made is hardly comparable to initial action.

To some extent, moreover, Dean Coleman's announcement may have operated as a challenge that helped turn part of the crowd from interested bystanders into sit-in demonstrators. A University press release announced that the decision to order the students to leave Hamilton Hall came after the students had decided to stage a sit-in.

Dean Coleman's testimony, however, makes no mention of any prior student decision to sit-in and the sequence of events strongly suggests that there could have been none until Dean Platt finished talking to the lawyers and parents. The group in Hamilton Hall was uncertain what action was being taken with respect to the four SDS students who refused to appear. Many people even thought decision had been postponed until the next morning. Assuredly there was no sit-in demonstration up to that point. Dean Platt went directly from his meeting with the parents to Hamilton Hall. When he got there, he was told that the decision had already been made to send Dean Coleman with the order to the students. There can hardly have been time for the students to decide to sit-in and news of their decision to reach the Administration while Dean Platt was walking from Hamilton Hall to Low Library. Dean Coleman's order, therefore, seems to have directed the students to leave the building under threat of suspension and police action at a time when they might have left anyway; it thus offered SDS a new opportunity for another dramatic showdown.

But even though there is room for misgiving, the Administration's decision to direct the students to leave is understandable. In April the scale of disturbances had mounted as the result of patient efforts to avoid a showdown. Recollection of the unhappy consequences of that delay must have pressed those charged with the decision upon the opposite horn of the dilemma.

The third critical point was the decision to clear the campus during the early morning of May 21. The existence of turmoil as Hamilton Hall was cleared is undisputed. Dean Platt thought that it was dying down and would gradually wear itself out. President Kirk and his associates inside Low Library thought the risks of delay were too great to postpone drastic measures. We have no basis for second guessing those on the scene, although we feel obliged to repeat our earlier observation that there is grave danger of exaggerating the willingness and ability of a police force to take effective action against many hundreds in a time of intense emotion, without resorting to violence. When so many are involved, calling upon the police to intervene is rarely the end of the matter.

We have canvassed these issues without reaching firm conclusions for two reasons. First, the canvass may be of value to those who seek lessons in experience. Second, for the future of Columbia University it is important to recognize that these were subtle issues with wide ramifications to which there were and are no clear-cut answers. With that realization may come both a degree of tolerance for those who had to act despite their doubts and a degree of open-mindedness in reexamining any decisions that are not irretrievable.

PART THREE

GENERAL
OBSERVATIONS

I

The April uprising started and grew haphazardly. As it developed to the final academic cataclysm, its entire character was altered.

The long series of turbulent demonstrations beginning in 1965, which were tolerated by most of the University community, leaves a tragic sense of the inevitability of the final escalation. Packing the lobby of Hamilton Hall—even the somewhat ambiguous obstruction of Dean Coleman's liberty—was scarcely different from the earlier confrontation in John Jay Hall or the sit-in following the CIA demonstration. SAS's decision to evict the whites and barricade the doors in a demonstration of black student power—one of the key turning points—was a response to an occasion thrust upon the black students. With each successive day the uprising gathered its own physical and emotional momentum.

We reject the view that ascribes the April and May disturbances primarily to a conspiracy of student revolutionaries. That demonology is no less false than the naive radical doctrine that attributes all wars, racial injustices, and poverty to the machinations of a capitalist and militarist "Establishment." Student revolutionists within SDS planned turbulent confrontations and revolutionary tactics. They manipulated facts in ways that created distrust and bred unwarranted antagonism. There apparently was occasional talk of wider revolution to overthrow the present political system. A very few revolutionists may have been in dead earnest. More, we suspect, were half in dreamland, feverishly discussing romantic tactics but hardly contemplating realistic execution. Part of the responsibility for the disturbances rests upon the revolutionaries consciously seeking to subvert and destroy the University but their total number was small—much less than the full SDS membership— and their activities were only the catalyst that precipitated a deeper movement.*

II

By its final days the revolt enjoyed both wide and deep support among the students and junior faculty and in lesser degree among the senior professors. The grievances of the rebels were felt equally by a still larger number, probably a majority, of the students. The trauma of the violence that followed police intervention intensified emotions but support for the demonstrators rested upon broad discontent and widespread sympathy for their position.

The record contains ample proof of this conclusion. The very number of students arrested in the buildings—524 Columbia students in the first police action—is convincing. Many more had been in the buildings earlier. Some of the latter were doubtless curiosity seekers. For others in both groups the affair probably had many of the elements of the once-traditional spring riots and subsequent "panty raids." But even after discount is made for those elements, the extent of active participation in violent and unlawful protest is significant.

The existence of broad underlying unrest is also shown by the progress of the seizures. The action of the black students in Hamilton Hall was entirely independent of SDS. The seizure of Avery Hall by architectural students was their own movement. The occupation of Fayerweather Hall, in which a large part of graduate study in the social sciences is centered, was

---

* By the same token our comments concerning the above group should not be applied to the much larger number who seek fundamental change in the established order without embracing doctrinaire revolutionary theory and tactics.

apparently spontaneous; no evidence of an SDS connection has come to our attention.

Outside the buildings the militants enjoyed visible support in the form of the thousands who watched from various points on campus, most conspicuously at the Sundial. A campus poll reportedly boycotted by those in the buildings showed that 74 percent of the participants favored "end gym construction," 66 percent favored severing ties with IDA, and 37 percent even favored amnesty for all students involved in the demonstrations.

The events after the police "bust" point to the same conclusion. The emotions excited by the brutality must have polarized opinion. There would be a tendency to put unjust blame upon those who called for police intervention rather than those—chiefly from SDS—whose deliberate efforts to provoke disruptive turbulence made it almost inevitable that police action would be required. Despite these complex cross-currents, the extent and persistence of the ultimate reaction against the University Administration is adequately explained only by the presence of strong but latent dissatisfaction quickened by the violence of events.

For the future it is equally important to note that the support for the activists has come from the portions of the student body who are most energetically concerned with university and community affairs.

III

The avowed objectives of the April demonstrations, stripped of their context and symbolism, were inadequate causes for an uprising.

The University's IDA affiliation had little practical importance. It was being reviewed by the Henkin Committee as part of a larger study of Columbia's relations to outside agencies. There was not the slightest reason to doubt that the normal academic procedures could produce a reasoned and fair-minded decision upon the merits. The disruptive potential of the IDA affiliation at Columbia, as at other universities, was that it enabled the large part of the intellectual community, especially students, to transfer to the campus their intense moral indignation against the Vietnam war.

The gymnasium issue was more complex, but it too was a symbolic issue. At least some black students freely acknowledge not only that the issue was oversimplified but that the public gymnasium to be built by Columbia would be more beneficial to the community than the 2.1 acres of rocky parkland, *if* the project could be judged upon that aspect alone. But the project could not be judged out of the context of Columbia's relations with its poorer neighbors and society's treatment of racial ghettos.

The third issue, the discipline of the six IDA demonstrators, had somewhat greater substance. Although most students would probably have agreed that the disruptive manner of conducting SDS demonstrations was becoming intolerable, many students were antagonized by the manner in which the "no indoor demonstration" rule was promulgated and the discipline was administered.

Since the rule came close to the area of free expression staunchly guarded by Columbia's liberal tradition, it was of intense concern to the entire University community. Nevertheless, the prohibition was promulgated by President Kirk without consultation with students, and apparently without prior discussion with faculty members. In fact, the rule ran contrary to the unanimous recommendation of a tripartite committee whose report the President withheld.

The rule, which was an obvious target for militants, was formulated in terms that hampered consistent administration and invited provocation.

Out of the 100 students who engaged in the March IDA demonstration, six SDS leaders were selected for punishment. It was difficult to persuade students that this was not a discriminatory selection even though the Dean's office explained that these six and no others were recognized.

The six IDA demonstrators were refused a public hearing and peremptorily punished. Although the older paternalistic procedures probably gave much greater protection to most student offenders, there is wide and justified campus support for the principles (1) that a student is no less entitled to due process of law than one charged with a public offense and (2) that students should share in disciplinary procedures as part of the right of participation in decisions affecting their interests.

IV

Three among the purely internal causes of unrest especially impressed us.

1. At a time when the spirit of self-determination is running strongly, the administration of Columbia's affairs too often conveyed an attitude of authoritarianism and invited distrust. In part, the appearance resulted from style: for example, it gave affront to read that an influential University official was no more interested in student opinion on matters of intense concern to students than he was in their taste for strawberries. In part, the appearance reflected the true state of affairs. The machinery of student government had been allowed to deteriorate to a point where Columbia College had no student government. The Report on Student Life was not released for seven months until CUSC members threatened publication. The President was unwilling to surrender absolute disciplinary powers. In addition, government by improvisation seems to have been not an exception, but the rule.

2. The quality of student life was inferior in living conditions and personal association.

3. Columbia, like other universities, has scarcely faced the extraordinary difficulties that face black students in the transition from a society permeated by racial injustice to one of true equality of opportunity. We recognize, of course, the difficulty of immediately remedying such deficiencies as the paucity of black teaching and administrative personnel and of appropriate courses and counseling for all students, but the indisputable fact of alienation of our black students, with all that that fact entails, makes a more active and creative search for solutions particularly urgent.

V

The fabric of Columbia was twisted and torn by the forces of political and social revolution outside the University. Columbia's geographic situation symbolizes the relation between white and black, affluence and poverty, youthful reform and established order. The University's need for physical expansion in an urban center creates inescapable tensions but its relations with the community had further deteriorated because of its apparent indifference to the needs and aspirations of its poorer neighbors. The handling of the gymnasium controversy thus came, even somewhat unfairly, to epitomize the conflict between the spirit of the civil rights movement and the attack on poverty, on the one hand, and, on the other, the ways of an *ancien régime*. Energetic and idealistic students, alienated from the older generation by an extraordinarily wide gulf in manners and interests and offended by the plethora of human suffering, were drawn to the side of change. Where they were frustrated by the massive anonymity of the government and the unmanageability of the social system, they could strike out at the more vulnerable University.

In like fashion, the University became the surrogate for all the tensions and frustrations of United States policy in Vietnam.

The desire for student power, while scarcely articulated as a cause for seizing the campus buildings, was a powerful element of the explosion. Discussion since the uprising has focused upon the methods by which students may exert more influence upon the government of an institution of which they are vital and integral parts. Participation in self-government is a natural human desire that today's students feel with greater urgency, particularly at institutions with highly selective admissions policies because they are much better educated than their predecessors, more sophisticated, in many respects more mature, and more interested in social problems than seeking out conventional careers. (Unfortunately, they are also much less disciplined.)

VI

The hurricane of social unrest struck Columbia at a time when the University was deficient in the cement that binds an institution into a cohesive unit.

Again, geography is a factor. The competing attractions

of the exciting metropolitan area, coupled with the housing problems that induce a majority of the faculty to live outside Manhattan, operate as centrifugal forces. Yet the dispirited quality of student life outside the classroom is not beyond the University's power of influence.

The formal organization of both the administrative offices and the faculties apparently tends to discourage the cohesiveness that comes from shared responsibility in matters of university concern. We were struck by the constant recital of an apposition between the Administration and the faculty as rival bodies with separate interests, for it would seem to us that on educational questions the two should be essentially one. The lack of a University Senate and the division of the professors and other teachers into three or four faculties—quite apart from the professional schools—where other universities have a single Faculty of Arts and Sciences, apparently discourages faculty participation in the formulation of University policy and the improvement of student life. The central Administration to which the full burden of the quality of student life is left is not equipped for the duty. Far too few members of the University family are closely involved, outside the classroom, in the constant informal enterprises and discussions by which the values of an academic community are constantly reexamined and those which stand the test are passed on to the next generation.

Institutional coherence is also affected by the presence or lack of a spirit of institutional self-confidence. Unhappily, despite her inherent strengths, the spring crisis struck Columbia when her self-confidence was shaken by the decline in relative position in AAUP rankings of graduate departments, the exclusion from a Ford Foundation grant for improvement of graduate studies, the resignations of a number of senior professors, and the Strickman filter incident.

VII

The scale of the disturbances was greatly enlarged in numbers, intensity and violence by the delay in calling the police—from Thursday night until Monday night—which the

Ad Hoc Faculty Group forced upon the University officials. Although perhaps the effort had to be made, there was
never a significant chance that the Group could negotiate a
peaceful withdrawal from the buildings. Forcing the delay,
by threats of physical interposition, increased the likelihood of
violence and magnified the reaction by lending an air of legitimacy to use of the tactics of physical disruption as means of
forcing one view of policy upon those who held another.

VIII

Our next five observations must be taken as a unit. Language requires stating them one at a time, but none can
survive unless joined with the others.

A.

A university is essentially a free community of scholars
dedicated to the pursuit of truth and knowledge solely through
reason and civility.

A privately-endowed university depends upon the experienced guidance of wise counselors and managers both inside
and outside academic ranks, and also upon the financial and
moral support of a large, organized body of alumni and
friends. But their vital contribution must never obscure the
essential quality of the institution: the university is a community of scholars, both teachers and students. Any tendency
to treat a university as business enterprise with faculty as
employees and students as customers diminishes its vitality
and communal cohesion.

B.

Resort to violence or physical harassment or obstruction is
never an acceptable tactic for influencing decisions in a university. This principle does not require notions of property or
legality to sustain it. It derives from three considerations.

First, force, harassment, and physical obstruction * contra-

---

* For an explanation of the sense in which we use the above
terms, see the footnote on page 27.

dict the essential postulate that the university is dedicated to the search for truth by reason and civility.

Second, resort to such physical coercion tends to set in motion an uncontrollable escalation of violence. This is the plainest lesson of the rising cycle of violence that began at Columbia with the Naval ROTC demonstration in 1965 and culminated in the brutality of April 30 and May 22. The sequence of steps was not inevitable but each was the readily predictable consequence of those that went before.

Third, the survival—literally the survival—of the free university depends upon the entire community's active rejection of disruptive demonstrations. Any sizeable group, left to pursue such tactics, can destroy either the university by repeatedly disrupting its normal activities or the university's freedom by compelling the authorities to invoke overwhelming force in order that its activities may continue. The only alternative is for the entire community to reject the tactics of physical disruption with such overwhelming moral disapproval as to make them self-defeating.

This vital decision rests with the liberal and reform-minded students. They can save or destroy the institution.

C.

The acceptability of the foregoing principle depends upon organization of the scholarly community in ways that produce both loyalty and the relief of grievances. The government of a university depends, even more than that of a political community, upon the consent of all the governed to accept decisions reached by its constitutional processes. The consent of the dissenters depends partly upon their knowing that their views effectively entered into the process of consensus, even though they did not prevail. They must also be convinced that the opportunities for change are open and the goals and stance of the enterprise are sufficiently right for it to deserve their loyalty despite specific points of disagreement. Administrative intractability and resistance to change contribute to the breakdown of law and order.

D.

The student body is a mature and essential part of the community of scholars. This principle has more validity today than ever before in history. It is felt more keenly by a wider number of students, perhaps because of the increasing democratization of human institutions. As with all human activities, the wise division of functions and responsibilities must take into account the special skills or limitations of particular groups, as well as efficiency of operation. The process of drawing students into more vital participation in the governance of the university is infinitely complex. It cannot be resolved by either abstractions or tables of organization. It does not mean that issues must be settled by referenda. *We are convinced, however, that ways must be found, beginning now, by which students can meaningfully influence the education afforded them and other aspects of the university activities.*

The activist supporters of reform who voiced the grievances pressed by the rebels included many of the natural leaders among students—both political and intellectual leaders. They were deeply hurt by statements treating them merely as disloyal trouble-makers aligned with a small band of rebels. While their own releases, for reasons of student politics, contributed to the polarization of opinion by their lack of civility, we have not the slightest doubt that the survival of Columbia as a leading university depends upon finding ways of drawing this very large and constructive segment of the student body, which supported the strike, back into the stream of university life where it can share in the process of rebuilding.

With participation, students will surely acquire a more sophisticated understanding of the universities' difficulties and complexities and of the necessary functions of the faculty and administration, the alumni, and the governing body. In the same process, the latter would come to an understanding they cannot otherwise acquire of the true needs and aspirations of students and values and shortcomings of current educational measures.

E.

We add only that the success of those who must follow this difficult course will depend in no small measure upon the willingness of parents, alumni, and friends to recognize that the April crisis is thus being converted into a creative source of renewal.

APPENDIX A

PRINCIPAL PARTICIPANTS IN THE COLUMBIA DISTURBANCES CITED IN THE REPORT

ADMINISTRATION

Thomas S. Colahan, Vice-Dean, Columbia College

Henry S. Coleman, Acting Dean, Columbia College

Andrew W. Cordier, Dean, School of International Affairs

Herbert A. Deane, Vice-Dean, Graduate Faculties and sometime Acting-Dean

George K. Fraenkel, Dean, Graduate Faculties

Warren F. Goodell, Vice-President for Administration

Ralph S. Halford, Assistant to the President for Special Projects, formerly Dean of the Graduate Faculties

William E. Kahn, Proctor of the University

Grayson Kirk, President, Columbia University

Thomas A. McGoey, Vice-President for Business

H. Houston Merrit, Dean, School of Medicine

Alexander B. Platt, Associate Dean for Student Affairs, Columbia College

David B. Truman, Vice-President and Provost, formerly Dean of Columbia College

FACULTY AND RELATED INDIVIDUALS

Quentin Anderson, Professor of English, Co-Chairman of the Joint Discipline Committee

Daniel Bell, Professor of Sociology

John D. Cannon, University Chaplain, Chairman of the President's Committee on Religious Life

Eugene Galanter, Professor of Psychology

A. Bruce Goldman, Counselor to Jewish Students

Richard L. Greeman, Instructor in French

Marvin Harris, Professor of Anthropology

C. Lowell Harriss, Professor of Economics

Louis Henkin, Hamilton Fish Professor of International Law and Diplomacy, Chairman of the Committee on External Ties

Carl F. Hovde, Associate Professor of English

Serge Lang, Professor of Mathematics

Sidney Morgenbesser, Professor of Philosophy

Philip E. Mosely, Professor of International Relations, Director of the European Institute

Orest A. Ranum, Associate Professor of History

David J. Rothman, Associate Professor of History

Warner Schilling, Professor of Government

Allan A. Silver, Associate Professor of Sociology and Chairman Committee on Recruiting

William F. Starr, Counselor to Protestant Students

Lionel Trilling, George Edward Woodberry Professor of Literature and Criticism

Immanuel Wallerstein, Associate Professor of Sociology, Chairman of the Faculty Civil Rights Committee

Aaron W. Warner, Professor of Human Relations, Chairman of the Student Life Committee

Alan F. Westin, Professor of Public Law and Government, Chairman of the Ad Hoc Faculty Group

NEIGHBORHOOD LEADERS

Amelia Betanzos, Democratic District Leader, Chairman of the Ad Hoc Committee on Morningside Park

Patrick Cronan, Republican District Leader, Vice-Chairman of the Ad Hoc Committee on Morningside Park

J. Raymond Jones, Democratic Leader

Charles 37x Kenyatta, Harlem Mau Mau

Robert McKay, Member, West Harlem Morningside Park Committee

Joseph Monroe, Member, West Harlem Morningside Park Committee

Basil Patterson, State Senator

Charles Rangel, State Assemblyman

A. Kuchel Smith, Minister, Harlem pastor

Percy Sutton, former State Assemblyman, Manhattan Borough President

POLICE

Harcourt Dodds, Deputy Commissioner
Sanford Garelick, Chief Inspector
James Taylor, Deputy Chief Inspector
Eldridge Waith, Assistant Chief Inspector
John Walsh, First Deputy Commissioner

POLITICIANS

William Booth, Commissioner of the City Commission on
 Human Rights
Sid Davidoff, Assistant to the Mayor
Barry Gottehrer, Assistant to the Mayor
Thomas P. Hoving, former Commissioner of the Department of
 Parks
Jay Kriegel, Assistant to the Mayor
Newbold Morris, former Commissioner of the Department of
 Parks
Robert Moses, former Commissioner of the Department of Parks
William Fitz Ryan, Congressman

STUDENTS

Ray Brown, member, SAS
Jay Dobkin, Chairman, Citizenship Council, 1967–1968
Nicholas Freudenberg, member SDS
Ted Gold, Vice-Chairman, SDS, 1967–68
Juan Gonzalez, member, Strike Coordinating Committee
Ted Kaptchuk, Chairman, SDS, 1967–68
Mark Rudd, Chairman, SDS, 1968–
Paul Vilardi, Chairman, Majority Coalition
Cicero Wilson, President, SAS
Joel Ziff, Chairman, Citizenship Council, 1968–1969

TRUSTEES

Harold F. McGuire, Vice-Chairman, Board of Trustees; Chairman of the University Gymnasium Committee
William E. Petersen, Chairman, Board of Trustees

TEXT OF OCTOBER PROPOSALS
FOR DEMONSTRATIONS
AT COLUMBIA

POSITION PAPER ON STRATEGY FOR REST OF YEAR—
UNIVERSITY COMPLICITY

Now that we have presented our demands to Kirk, and confronted the war-makers in Washington, we are faced with the problem of what to do. What to do, that is, to achieve our two basic goals:

1. The "radicalization" of students—showing people the connections in the liberal structure, showing them how our lives really are unfree in this society (and at Columbia), getting them to act in their own interest, and

2. Striking a blow at the Federal Government's war effort ("resistance").

The two goals are intimately connected in a theory-practice relationship with the university and [students] will become conscious of their own interests and needs and the way the university acts against them, corrupting and distorting education in a bewildering variety of forms (paternalism, complicity with the war, career orientation, pedantry, bureaucracy). We will be able to present our alternative to this university and this society as we discuss the role of the university under capitalism.

In short, "radicalization" is developed by both working toward an objective goal—severing university ties to the war—and the consciousness S.D.S. as leadership injects into the struggle.

But in order to accomplish more than the posture of radical action (e.g., to be more than a bloody, disorganized march on Washington), we're going to have to develop the two things which we most lack now—a coherent strategy, and an effective organization. To be militant is to fight to achieve a specific goal:

Let us clearly state that our goal is to end university complicity with the war: I.D.A. [Institute for Defense Analyses], N.R.O.T.C., C.I.A. contracts, recruiting, etc.

But we can never force the university to submit to our demands unless we have behind us the strength of the majority of students on campus. We can achieve this majority at Columbia, where over half of the students "are against the war," but we will need real organizational strength to mobilize these people. We have the potential for such strength; what's lacking now is strategy and commitment to the work necessary to win.

The following is a strategy, step by step, which we should follow.

PHASE I. DECISION AND POSITION. NOVEMBER

A committee elected by the general assembly draws up a statement of general strategy (goals of the campaign, its organization, and the range of its tactics), and a position paper (a very broad theoretical statement of S.D.S.'s objections to the Federal presence). These statements should be discussed and adopted by the general assembly as official guidelines for the campaign. The organization should be discussed and the structure laid out.

PHASE II. ORGANIZATION AND TRAINING. NOVEMBER-DECEMBER

A research committee prepares a 10 or 15 page factual paper with bibliography for the dorm canvassers. The dorm organization is constructed, with a committee for each dorm. Canvassers discuss arguments they will probably encounter in their work, as well. The research committee should also assemble the material it will need to provide a steady stream of propaganda and exposures during the next phases.

Secretarial committee works on the mailing list (a big job). The defense squad begins training. Financial and faculty support are sought.

Action: Begin circulation of a petition on our demands, prove action against R.O.T.C. classes, harassment of recruiters (obstructing them without being liable to official retaliation), a few dormitory programs.

A committee should produce a manifesto giving our analysis of an alternative to the university. This should provide a second front for discussion, complementing that of opposition to the war. Liaison should be set up with other I.D.A. campuses as well as other N.Y.C. campuses for support and coordination.

PHASE III. MASS BASE. JANUARY-FEBRUARY

Intensive dorm canvassing, debates, discussions, and newspaper propaganda, in preparation for a C.U.S.C. [Columbia University Student Council] referendum on university complicity scheduled for about March 10. Spontaneous demonstrations around campus. Publication of more material on goals, demands, and their justifications.

Harassment of recruiters, R.O.T.C. to continue. Publication of all Federal projects with a list of their personnel. A fund-raising rally to be held.

PHASE IV. PREPARATION FOR MASS ACTION. MARCH

Presentation of huge petition to the university. A rally two days before the referendum. March 10—the referendum, which we will win, if we've done our work right. March 15, rally at which we issue final ultimatum: university must consider referendum binding and must meet our demands by April 5. Individuals will sign a pledge to militant action if the demands are not met.

PHASE V. MASS ACTION. APRIL

A sit in at Low Library which, after one day, turns into a general student strike. University capitulates.

April 24, 1968

To the Columbia University Students in Hamilton Hall:

This is to state that the disciplinary action taken against the students presently occupying Hamilton Hall will be disciplinary probation for the academic year 1968–1969 and the remainder of the present academic year, if you leave by 10 P.M. tonight and, when leaving the building, supply your name by signature. Criminal charges will not be pressed if the above conditions are met.

In view of the action taken by the Columbia College Faculty, the President plans to ask the Chairman of the Trustees to call a special meeting of the board at the earliest practicable time to consider the Faculty recommendations concerning the gymnasium.

ALEXANDER B. PLATT
Associate Dean
Columbia College

APPENDIX D

April 25, 1968

TO: The Columbia Students in Hamilton Hall

This is to inform you that I shall recommend favorably to the Trustees motion five passed by the Faculty of Columbia College on 24 April. The text of the motion is:

That this Faculty respectfully petitions the University Administration

a) to arrange the immediate suspension of on-site excavation of the gymnasium facility in Morningside Park.

b) to be prepared to review the matter of the gymnasium site with a group of community spokesmen; the administration will immediately invite the Mayor to designate a group who will take counsel with the University with respect to the location and character of the gymnasium.

Your attention is especially drawn to Part B of this motion. In order to make explicit the character and purposes of the group to be designated by the Mayor, I shall recommend to the Trustees that the Mayor be asked to secure the approval of leaders acceptable to the Harlem Community of the group's composition, procedures and powers.

If you will leave Hamilton Hall, your names will be taken and you will receive a disciplinary warning for the remainder of the academic year 1967–68 and for the academic year 1968–69. No criminal charges will be made against any person presently in Hamilton Hall. Even with this warning you may participate in all College and University extra-curricular activities, including the Student Afro-American Society. At the conclusion of a student's period on disciplinary warning no permanent record or physical evidence of such status will remain in his record.

GRAYSON KIRK
President

April 24, 1968

Mr. Edward B. McMenamin
Secretary of the University
208 Low Memorial Library

Dear Mr. McMenamin:

At the special meeting of the Faculty of Columbia College on April 24, 1968, the following resolutions were proposed and approved:

1. That a University exists as a community dedicated to rational discourse, and the use of communication and persuasion as the means of furthering that discourse.

2. That this Faculty endorses the right to protest, but strongly condemns both obstructive behavior and physical violence on this campus. In this light we deplore the use of coercion, and the seizure of Dean Coleman as a hostage. Further we condemn the act of invasion of the President's Office and the rifling of his files.

3. That we believe that any differences have to be settled peacefully, and we trust that police action will not be used to clear Hamilton Hall or any other University building.

4. That to the extent that the issues which have arisen in the University community are due to a failure of communication and discussion within the University, we call upon the Administration to set up a tripartite body to discuss any disciplinary matters arising out of the incidents yesterday and today, the issue of the gymnasium and any other matters which are subjects of legitimate concern to the University community.

5. That this Faculty respectfully petitions the University administration

    a. to arrange the immediate suspension of on-site excavation of the gymnasium facility in Morningside Park.

b. to be prepared to review the matter of the gymnasium site with a group of community spokesmen; the administration will immediately invite the Mayor to designate a group who will take counsel with the University with respect to the location and character of the gymnasium.

Respectfully submitted,

JOSEPH L. BLAU

Secretary of the Faculty

(Note from the Dean: I wish to make absolutely clear that in passing resolution number 4 the Faculty reaffirmed that discipline is the responsibility of the President of the University, subject to delegation to the Dean of the College.

The Trustees alone can act on resolution number 5. President Kirk will ask the Chairman of the Board of Trustees to call a special meeting of the Board to consider this matter.

—Henry S. Coleman)

RESOLUTION OF THE AD HOC
FACULTY GROUP

28 April 1968

We believe that there is a fundamental crisis which is shaking the foundations of this University and that thus far no solution has been found. The Ad Hoc Faculty Group proposes what we believe may be the last possibility of peaceful settlement.

I.   We recommend that the President establish the Tripartite Commission in the form defined in the report of the Ad Hoc Committee composed of Professors Galanter, Hovde and Trilling.

We recommend that the University statutes be revised by the Trustees so that the Tripartite Commission serve as the body of ultimate judicial review on all matters affecting University discipline.

We believe that the dimensions and complexity of the current crisis demand that a new approach of collective responsibility be adopted, and in this light insist that uniform penalties be applied to all violators of the discipline of the University.

II.   All excavation work at the gymnasium site having been suspended, we now recommend that the Trustees at their next meeting, which we urge occur within three days, request the Mayor of the City of New York urgently to convene a panel composed of:
a. representatives of the Trustees,
b. representatives of the Community appointed by the Mayor,
c. representatives of the Faculty to be chosen by the Faculty themselves.

We recommend that this panel review the gymnasium and adopt an alternative to the present plans. Should the alternative involve remaining on the present site, this plan shall be acceptable to the representatives of the Community.

III.   We request that once the President indicates that he accepts these resolutions as his recommendations to the Trustees, we call upon the students now improperly occupying various buildings to vacate these buildings immediately and to submit themselves to due process as shall now be established.

IV.   These proposals being in our judgment a just solution to the crisis our University is presently undergoing, we pledge that
    a. If the President will not adopt these proposals, we shall take all measures within our several consciences to prevent the use of force to vacate these buildings.
    b. If the President does accept our proposals but the students in the buildings refuse to evacuate these buildings, we shall refuse further to interpose ourselves between the Administration and the students.

V.   We cannot believe that the Trustees, charged with the welfare of all segments of the University, will not accept a solution regarded as just by students, faculty, and the President.

VI.   As members of the faculty, we are determined to do everything within our power rapidly to resume the full life of this institution in the firm expectation that our proposals will permit a climate to prevail that will once again allow reason, judgment and order to reign.

RESOLUTION PASSED AT SPECIAL MEETING OF ALL FACULTIES OF THE UNIVERSITY ON MORNINGSIDE HEIGHTS, SUNDAY, APRIL 28, 1968

1) We reaffirm the actions taken by the faculty of Columbia College on April 24 and in the Committees on Instruction of the Graduate Faculties meeting jointly on April 26. With them

a) we condemn the violence that has occurred, including the occupation of buildings and the disruption of normal University activities;

b) we commend the action of the administration in arranging immediate suspension of on-site excavation for the gymnasium in Morningside Park, and we urge that it proceed at once to meet with community spokesmen to review the matter of the gymnasium site;

c) we endorse the establishment of a tripartite commission, and express the conviction that its work can result in a fair disposition of the disciplinary problems arising from the current disruption and in progress toward solution of other issues lying within its jurisdiction.

2) We express our deep appreciation of the patience and restraint shown by the administration and by the great majority of our faculty and students.

3) We recognize that members of the ad hoc faculty group meeting in 301 Philosophy have performed many vital services in the interest of this University. We hope they will continue their effective efforts at communication and mediation.

4) We are convinced that significant progress has been made toward closer communication among students, faculty,

and administration in recent days and we pledge our efforts to make this a permanent feature of the University's life.

5) We likewise pledge our efforts to effective, continuing communication with the broader community of which we are a part.

6) We call upon the students who continue to occupy University buildings to recognize that failure to resolve this crisis rapidly and peaceably may result in irreparable damage to all members of this community.

COLUMBIA UNIVERSITY
JOINT COMMITTEE
ON DISCIPLINARY AFFAIRS

APPEAL OF AB

In a letter dated May 16, 1968, Alex Platt, Associate Dean of Columbia College, charged AB with participation in the campus demonstrations beginning April 23 and requested AB to come to see him "on Tuesday afternoon, May 21, 1968, no later than 5:00 P.M." Dean Platt added: "In accordance with the recommendation of the Joint Committee on Disciplinary Affairs, I should inform you that if you fail to come in to see me by the above date, you shall be suspended from the University." AB did not go to see Dean Platt as requested, and by letter dated May 22, 1968 Dean Platt informed AB that he was suspended from the University. AB filed an appeal with the Joint Committee on June 13, 1968, challenging the propriety of his suspension.

In its report of May 9, the Joint Committee recommended that "the Dean of each School or Faculty should determine which students in that School or Faculty were involved in the demonstrations and, following discussions with those students, should impose the discipline recommended above [disciplinary probation, in most instances]. A student who fails to appear before the Dean should be suspended." If the student denied the Dean's charges, he was entitled to a hearing before a disciplinary tribunal; the student also was entitled to a formal hearing if the Dean sought penalties more serious than disciplinary probation.

The report of May 9 was "predicated on the assumption that [criminal] trespass charges will be dropped." When it became evident from President Kirk's statement of May 9 and the

Trustees' statement of the same date that the criminal charges would not be dropped, the Joint Committee had to reconsider its position. In its report of May 13, the Joint Committee recommended that the "Deans begin to implement its recommendations concerning intramural discipline, but that application of all penalties be held in abeyance, pending action in the courts." The Joint Committee added: "A student who fails to appear before the Dean is liable to immediate suspension, even though a trespass charge is still pending against him."

Thus, it appears that Dean Platt's actions were in complete accord with the recommendations of the Joint Committee. What are the grounds of AB's appeal?

First, AB states that he was advised by his attorneys in the criminal trespass action not to appear before Dean Platt so long as the criminal case was pending, "since any such appearance might be prejudicial to my case." In a telegram to Dean Platt dated May 18, 1968, the lawyers stated that AB's appearance before Dean Platt would "(1) make a nullity of AB's constitutional rights and protections; (2) make Columbia University prosecutor in one instance and judge in another; (3) be contrary to common practice of staying administrative hearings pending disposition of criminal charges; and (4) be contrary to recognized concepts of fair play and justice."

The allegations of the telegram are somewhat vague; to the extent that they are comprehensible, they are lacking in substance. (1) The only constitutional rights that appear to be involved are those pertaining to double jeopardy and self-incrimination. Double jeopardy is not violated because a university imposes discipline for conduct which also results in criminal sanctions. And the Joint Committee's recommendations recognized the privilege against self-incrimination in the hearing process and did not prevent AB from claiming the privilege in his appearance before the Dean. (2) The prosecutor in the criminal case is the State of New York, acting on the complaint of the Trustees of Columbia University, while the judges in the University disciplinary proceedings are Deans, disciplinary tribunals and the Joint Committee. (3)

While it is common for administrative bodies to stay hearings pending disposition of criminal charges, this is not the invariable practice; nor is it mandatory. The University has an interest in the prompt conclusion of intramural disciplinary proceedings and is not obliged to stay its own hand until external judicial processes are concluded. (4) For the reasons previously indicated, the requirement that AB appear before Dean Platt was not contrary to recognized concepts of fair play and justice. Indeed, the opposite conclusion—that a student can obtain immunity from prompt University discipline if only his misconduct is sufficiently serious to invite criminal prosecution—is hard to take seriously.

AB had absolutely nothing to lose by appearing before Dean Platt. He could have denied the charges and insisted on a hearing before a disciplinary tribunal. He could have claimed his privilege against self-incrimination, which also would have resulted in a hearing before a disciplinary tribunal. Or he could have admitted the charges and sought to have Dean Platt limit the academic discipline to a relatively mild sanction. Only the last course could conceivably have prejudiced AB's position in the courts; and he was not obliged to take that course if he thought it unwise after discussing the matter with Dean Platt.

We conclude, then, that AB's refusal to appear before Dean Platt was wholly unjustified. The remaining question is whether a student may excuse his failure to comply with a University directive because he has received legal advice not to do so. The question hardly survives its statement. The University does not, and cannot, control the outside legal advisors to whom a student may turn. To say that the University's authority may be nullified by contrary advice from an outside lawyer is to say that the University has no authority at all. We reject the proposition.

Second, AB says that he was not aware of the Joint Committee's statement of May 13 and that, looking solely to the Joint Committee's report of May 9 and to the fact that criminal trespass charges had not been dropped, he believed that Dean

Platt was not acting consistently with the Joint Committee's recommendations. In their telegram to Dean Platt, AB's lawyers observed that "while you refer to the Joint Committee's recommendation at no time have you informed my client that the trespass charges will be dropped, which you know is the assumption upon which the Committee's recommendations are based." What is the relevance of this objection?

Whether Dean Platt was acting in conformity with the Joint Committee's recommendations was not a matter of consequence in relation to the objections made by AB's lawyers. All four objections posed by them would have had the same weight (or lack of weight) whether or not Dean Platt was complying with the Joint Committee's recommendations. In this connection, we note that AB says that he first became aware of our May 13 document on May 22. Yet he did not on that day or on any subsequent day endeavor to see Dean Platt to explain the source of his confusion. He did not file his appeal with this Committee until June 13, over three weeks after his alleged enlightenment.

Dean Platt stated that he was proceeding "in accordance with the recommendation of the Joint Committee"; AB states that he did not believe him. Dean Platt happened to be telling the truth, as AB could have verified by directing an inquiry to the Joint Committee. The Joint Committee's report of May 13 was not a secret document. It was released to the campus community on the date of its issuance, and a story based on the report appeared in *Spectator* on May 16. The *Spectator* story is not a model of clarity, but it did indicate that the Joint Committee had taken action following its report of May 9, and that this action had sought to achieve an accommodation between University disciplinary proceedings and the criminal trespass charges. In the absence of any official campus publication, *Spectator* is a normal source of information concerning actions of University bodies. AB refused to comply with Dean Platt's directives without making any effort to determine whether those directives were in accord with the recommendations of the Joint Committee. He made no inquiry either of Dean Platt or the Joint Committee. His lawyers' telegram to

Dean Platt was not an inquiry; nor was it a substitute for his appearance.

Most of the other grounds in AB's appeal are plainly without merit. That Dean Platt was not in his office at all times during the afternoon; that certain statements were or were not made to the students' parents after the 5:00 p.m. deadline; that Dean Platt may have made a noncommittal statement to a *Spectator* reporter on the afternoon of May 21—all of these are irrelevant to the failure of AB to appear at Dean Platt's office prior to 5:00 p.m. That other groups of students were treated differently in fixing deadlines to appear is also immaterial.

The Deans obviously have to have discretion to take account of differences in numbers of students, timing of events, and status of students (students on probation vs. students about to graduate). We note that there have been other students who have failed to appear before Deans, and that they also have been suspended.

On one point, however, there is substance to AB's claim that he was treated inequitably. Some 73 students were suspended in May for a variety of reasons relating to the campus demonstrations. All but a few of these were suspended as of May 31, 1968, although the grounds for their suspension existed at an earlier date. This had the effect of permitting these students to obtain academic credit for the spring semester, while AB and a few others who were suspended on May 22 lost all credit for the semester. Without imputing improper motives to anyone, it is clear that the result of these different actions was to work a substantial disparity in treatment among suspended students lacking any rational justification. Accordingly, we rule that AB's suspension should be made effective as of May 31, 1968, instead of May 22, and that notices to outside agencies about the May 22 suspension be rescinded. In all other respects, the appeal is denied.

One further matter deserves comment. Suspension may appear to be a severe penalty to impose on a student for failing to appear before a Dean. But AB was informed that this would be the consequence. It is impossible to conduct an orderly university, or to conduct orderly disciplinary proceedings within a university, if students remain free to defy university officials upon any grounds that they think proper. Suspension and expulsion are the only substantial sanctions available to the University, and unless the University shows that it is willing to employ those sanctions to achieve compliance with its lawful directives, individuals will remain free to disrupt University functions.

Even so, the penalty should not be more severe than necessary. If AB is now prepared to submit to the disciplinary processes of the University, and to abide by the University's procedures and regulations, he should state his position in a petition for reinstatement addressed to the Dean of Columbia College. We recommend that the Dean or Associate Dean Platt review AB's petition, if one is submitted promptly, and hold such discussions with AB as the Dean thinks desirable; if the Dean concludes that AB wishes to rejoin the University community on the above terms, the Dean should reinstate AB and permit the regular disciplinary processes to take their course with respect to all University charges pending against AB.

We adopt this view partly because there is the possibility that AB was actually confused about his obligation to see the Dean at the time he refused to see Dean Platt, even though we have found that his refusal was unjustified. We are also influenced by the fact that AB has filed an appeal with this Committee and has thereby shown some interest in following the University's disciplinary procedures. Our recommendation in this case should not be interpreted to mean that other suspended students should be given the same opportunity without regard to the surrounding circumstances.

Appeal denied, with one modification and one recommendation.

MEMBERS PRESENT: Messrs. Anderson, Robey, Weiner, Goldfarb, Weingrad, Kenen, Jones, Gaspar, Motley, Witkin, Wellington, Rapkin, and Mrs. Chesler.

Mr. Wellington does not concur in the Joint Committee on Disciplinary Affairs's recommendation.

Appeal received: June 13, 1968.
Appeal decided: June 27, 1968.

IN ORDER TO PROTECT, INSOFAR AS POSSIBLE, THE
CONFIDENTIAL CHARACTER OF DISCIPLINARY PRO-
CEEDINGS, THE JOINT COMMITTEE ON DISCIPLINARY
AFFAIRS DOES NOT EMPLOY THE NAMES OF INDIVIDUAL
STUDENTS IN ISSUING ITS DECISIONS.